William Shakespeare (bapt. 26 April 1564 – 23 April 1616) was an English poet, playwright and actor, widely regarded as the greatest writer in the English language and the world's greatest dramatist. He is often called England's national poet and the "Bard of Avon". His extant works, including collaborations, consist of approximately 39 plays, 154 sonnets, two long narrative poems, and a few other verses, some of uncertain authorship. His plays have been translated into every major living language and are performed more often than those of any other playwright. Shakespeare was born and raised in Stratford-upon-Avon, Warwickshire. At the age of 18, he married Anne Hathaway, with whom he had three children: Susanna and twins Hamnet and Judith. Sometime between 1585 and 1592, he began a successful career in London as an actor, writer, and part-owner of a playing company called the Lord Chamberlain's Men, later known as the King's Men. At age 49 (around 1613), he appears to have retired to Stratford, where he died three years later. (Source: Wikipedia)

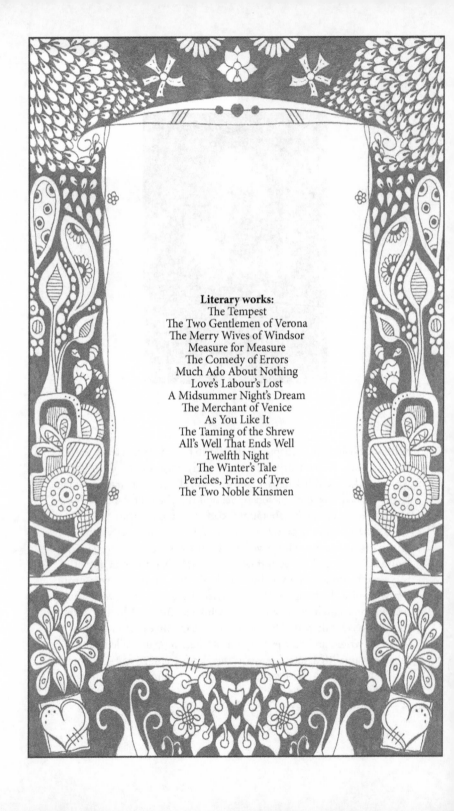

Literary works:
The Tempest
The Two Gentlemen of Verona
The Merry Wives of Windsor
Measure for Measure
The Comedy of Errors
Much Ado About Nothing
Love's Labour's Lost
A Midsummer Night's Dream
The Merchant of Venice
As You Like It
The Taming of the Shrew
All's Well That Ends Well
Twelfth Night
The Winter's Tale
Pericles, Prince of Tyre
The Two Noble Kinsmen

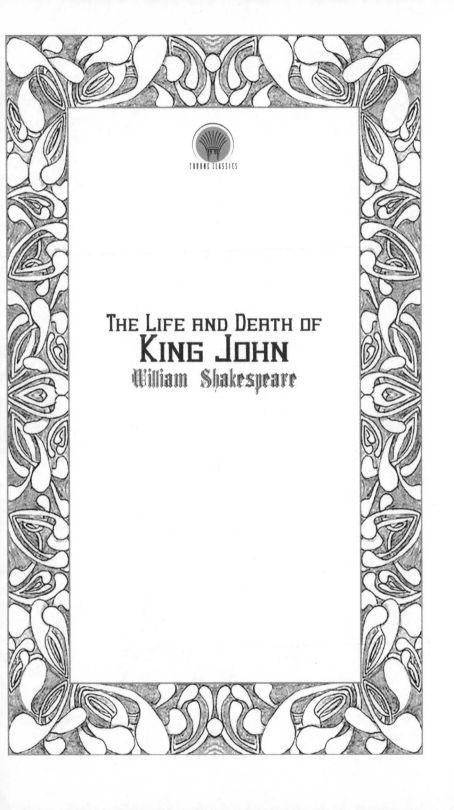

THRONE CLASSICS

THE LIFE AND DEATH OF
KING JOHN
William Shakespeare

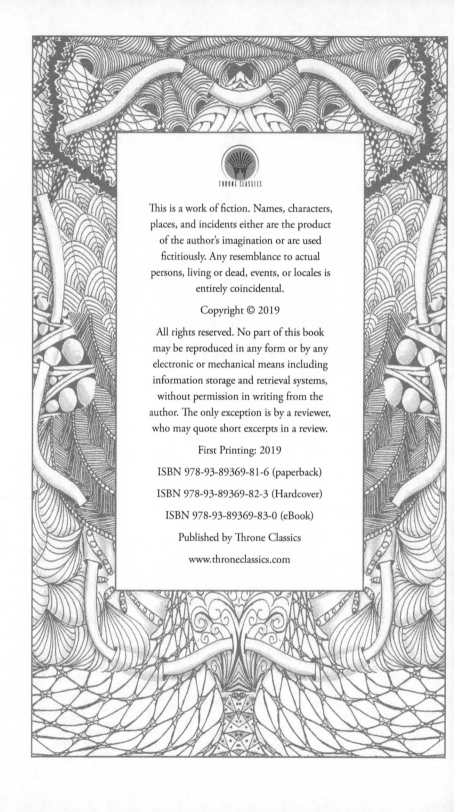

Copyright © 2019

First Printing: 2019

ISBN 978-93-89369-81-6 (paperback)

ISBN 978-93-89369-82-3 (Hardcover)

ISBN 978-93-89369-83-0 (eBook)

Published by Throne Classics

www.throneclassics.com

Contents

The Life and Death of
King John

PERSONS REPRESENTED

KING JOHN.

PRINCE HENRY, his son; afterwards KING HENRY III.

ARTHUR, Duke of Bretagne, son to GEFFREY, late Duke of Bretagne, the elder brother to King John.

WILLIAM MARSHALL, Earl of Pembroke.

GEOFFREY FITZ-PETER, Earl of Essex, Chief Justiciary of England.

WILLIAM LONGSWORD, Earl of Salisbury.

ROBERT BIGOT, Earl of Norfolk.

HUBERT DE BURGH, Chamberlain to the King.

ROBERT FALCONBRIDGE, son to Sir Robert Falconbridge.

PHILIP FALCONBRIDGE, his half-brother, bastard son to King Richard I.

JAMES GURNEY, servant to Lady Falconbridge.

PETER OF POMFRET, a prophet

PHILIP, King of France.

LOUIS, the Dauphin.

ARCHDUKE OF AUSTRIA.

CARDINAL PANDULPH, the Pope's legate.

MELUN, a French lord.

CHATILLON, Ambassador from France to King John.

ELINOR, Widow of King Henry II and Mother to King John.

CONSTANCE, Mother to Arthur.

BLANCH OF SPAIN, Daughter to Alphonso, King of Castile, and Niece

to King John.

LADY FALCONBRIDGE, Mother to the Bastard and Robert Falconbridge.

Lords, Citizens of Angiers, Sheriff, Heralds, Officers, Soldiers, Messengers, Attendants and other Attendants.

SCENE: England and France

ACT I.

SCENE 1. Northampton. A Room of State in the Palace.

[Enter KING JOHN, QUEEN ELINOR, PEMBROKE, ESSEX, SALISBURY, and others, with CHATILLON.]

KING JOHN.

Now, say, Chatillon, what would France with us?

CHATILLON.

Thus, after greeting, speaks the King of France,

In my behaviour, to the majesty,

The borrow'd majesty of England here.

ELINOR.

A strange beginning:—borrow'd majesty!

KING JOHN.

Silence, good mother; hear the embassy.

CHATILLON.

Philip of France, in right and true behalf

Of thy deceased brother Geffrey's son,

Arthur Plantagenet, lays most lawful claim

To this fair island and the territories,—

To Ireland, Poictiers, Anjou, Touraine, Maine;

Desiring thee to lay aside the sword

Which sways usurpingly these several titles,

And put the same into young Arthur's hand,

Thy nephew and right royal sovereign.

KING JOHN.

What follows if we disallow of this?

CHATILLON.

The proud control of fierce and bloody war,

To enforce these rights so forcibly withheld.

KING JOHN.

Here have we war for war, and blood for blood,

Controlment for controlment;—so answer France.

CHATILLON.

Then take my king's defiance from my mouth,

The farthest limit of my embassy.

KING JOHN.

Bear mine to him, and so depart in peace:

Be thou as lightning in the eyes of France;

For ere thou canst report I will be there,

The thunder of my cannon shall be heard:

So, hence! Be thou the trumpet of our wrath,

And sullen presage of your own decay.—

An honourable conduct let him have:—

Pembroke, look to 't. Farewell, Chatillon.

[Exeunt CHATILLON and PEMBROKE.]

ELINOR.

What now, my son! Have I not ever said

How that ambitious Constance would not cease

Till she had kindled France and all the world

Upon the right and party of her son?

This might have been prevented and made whole

With very easy arguments of love;

Which now the manage of two kingdoms must

With fearful bloody issue arbitrate.

KING JOHN.

Our strong possession and our right for us.

ELINOR.

Your strong possession much more than your right,

Or else it must go wrong with you and me:

So much my conscience whispers in your ear,

Which none but heaven and you and I shall hear.

[Enter the Sheriff of Northamptonshire, who whispers to Essex.]

ESSEX.

My liege, here is the strangest controversy,

Come from the country to be judg'd by you,

That e'er I heard: shall I produce the men?

KING JOHN.

Let them approach.—

[Exit SHERIFF.]

Our abbeys and our priories shall pay

This expedition's charge.

[Re-enter Sheriff, with ROBERT FAULCONBRIDGE and PHILIP, his bastard Brother.]

What men are you?

BASTARD.

Your faithful subject I, a gentleman

Born in Northamptonshire, and eldest son,

As I suppose, to Robert Falconbridge,—

A soldier by the honour-giving hand

Of Coeur-de-lion knighted in the field.

KING JOHN.

What art thou?

ROBERT.

The son and heir to that same Falconbridge.

KING JOHN.

Is that the elder, and art thou the heir?

You came not of one mother then, it seems.

BASTARD.

Most certain of one mother, mighty king,—

That is well known; and, as I think, one father:

But for the certain knowledge of that truth

I put you o'er to heaven and to my mother:—

Of that I doubt, as all men's children may.

ELINOR.

Out on thee, rude man! thou dost shame thy mother,

And wound her honour with this diffidence.

BASTARD.

I, madam? no, I have no reason for it,—

That is my brother's plea, and none of mine;

The which if he can prove, 'a pops me out

At least from fair five hundred pound a-year:

Heaven guard my mother's honour and my land!

KING JOHN.

A good blunt fellow.—Why, being younger born,

Doth he lay claim to thine inheritance?

BASTARD.

I know not why, except to get the land.

But once he slander'd me with bastardy:

But whe'er I be as true begot or no,

That still I lay upon my mother's head;

But that I am as well begot, my liege,—

Fair fall the bones that took the pains for me!—

Compare our faces and be judge yourself.

If old Sir Robert did beget us both,

And were our father, and this son like him,—

O old Sir Robert, father, on my knee

I give heaven thanks I was not like to thee!

KING JOHN.

Why, what a madcap hath heaven lent us here!

ELINOR.

He hath a trick of Coeur-de-lion's face;

The accent of his tongue affecteth him:

Do you not read some tokens of my son

In the large composition of this man?

KING JOHN.

Mine eye hath well examined his parts,

And finds them perfect Richard.—Sirrah, speak,

What doth move you to claim your brother's land?

BASTARD.

Because he hath a half-face, like my father;

With half that face would he have all my land:

A half-fac'd groat five hundred pound a-year!

ROBERT.

My gracious liege, when that my father liv'd,

Your brother did employ my father much,—

BASTARD.

Well, sir, by this you cannot get my land:

Your tale must be how he employ'd my mother.

ROBERT.

And once despatch'd him in an embassy

To Germany, there with the emperor

To treat of high affairs touching that time.

The advantage of his absence took the King,

And in the meantime sojourn'd at my father's;

Where how he did prevail I shame to speak,—

But truth is truth: large lengths of seas and shores

Between my father and my mother lay,—

As I have heard my father speak himself,—

When this same lusty gentleman was got.

Upon his death-bed he by will bequeath'd

His lands to me; and took it, on his death,

That this, my mother's son, was none of his;

And if he were, he came into the world

Full fourteen weeks before the course of time.

Then, good my liege, let me have what is mine,

My father's land, as was my father's will.

KING JOHN.

Sirrah, your brother is legitimate;

Your father's wife did after wedlock bear him;

And if she did play false, the fault was hers;

Which fault lies on the hazards of all husbands

That marry wives. Tell me, how if my brother,

Who, as you say, took pains to get this son,

Had of your father claim'd this son for his?

In sooth, good friend, your father might have kept

This calf, bred from his cow, from all the world;

In sooth, he might; then, if he were my brother's,

My brother might not claim him; nor your father,

Being none of his, refuse him. This concludes,—

My mother's son did get your father's heir;

Your father's heir must have your father's land.

ROBERT.

Shall then my father's will be of no force

To dispossess that child which is not his?

BASTARD.

Of no more force to dispossess me, sir,

Than was his will to get me, as I think.

ELINOR.

Whether hadst thou rather be a Falconbridge,

And like thy brother, to enjoy thy land,

Or the reputed son of Coeur-de-lion,

Lord of thy presence and no land beside?

BASTARD.

Madam, an if my brother had my shape

And I had his, Sir Robert's his, like him;

And if my legs were two such riding-rods,

My arms such eel-skins stuff'd, my face so thin

That in mine ear I durst not stick a rose

Lest men should say 'Look where three-farthings goes!'

And, to his shape, were heir to all this land,

Would I might never stir from off this place,

I would give it every foot to have this face;

I would not be Sir Nob in any case.

ELINOR.

I like thee well: wilt thou forsake thy fortune,

Bequeath thy land to him, and follow me?

I am a soldier, and now bound to France.

BASTARD.

Brother, take you my land, I'll take my chance:

Your face hath got five hundred pound a-year;

Yet sell your face for fivepence and 'tis dear.—

Madam, I'll follow you unto the death.

ELINOR.

Nay, I would have you go before me thither.

BASTARD.

Our country manners give our betters way.

KING JOHN.

What is thy name?

BASTARD.

Philip, my liege, so is my name begun;

Philip, good old Sir Robert's wife's eldest son.

KING JOHN.

From henceforth bear his name whose form thou bear'st:

Kneel thou down Philip, but rise more great,—

Arise Sir Richard and Plantagenet.

BASTARD.

Brother by the mother's side, give me your hand:

My father gave me honour, yours gave land.—

Now blessed be the hour, by night or day,

When I was got, Sir Robert was away!

ELINOR.

The very spirit of Plantagenet!—

I am thy grandam, Richard; call me so.

BASTARD.

Madam, by chance, but not by truth; what though?

Something about, a little from the right,

  In at the window, or else o'er the hatch;

Who dares not stir by day must walk by night;

  And have is have, however men do catch:

Near or far off, well won is still well shot;

And I am I, howe'er I was begot.

KING JOHN.

Go, Falconbridge; now hast thou thy desire:

A landless knight makes thee a landed squire.—

Come, madam,—and come, Richard; we must speed

For France, for France, for it is more than need.

BASTARD.

Brother, adieu. Good fortune come to thee!

For thou wast got i' th' way of honesty.

[Exeunt all but the BASTARD.]

A foot of honour better than I was;

But many a many foot of land the worse.

Well, now can I make any Joan a lady:—

'Good den, Sir Richard:'—'God-a-mercy, fellow:'—

And if his name be George, I'll call him Peter:

For new-made honour doth forget men's names:

'Tis too respective and too sociable

For your conversion. Now your traveller,—

He and his toothpick at my worship's mess;—

And when my knightly stomach is suffic'd,

Why then I suck my teeth, and catechize

My picked man of countries:—'My dear sir,'—

Thus leaning on mine elbow I begin,—

'I shall beseech you'—that is question now;

And then comes answer like an ABC-book:—

'O sir,' says answer 'at your best command;

At your employment; at your service, sir:'—

'No, sir,' says question 'I, sweet sir, at yours:

And so, ere answer knows what question would,—

Saving in dialogue of compliment,

And talking of the Alps and Apennines,

The Pyrenean and the river Po,—

It draws toward supper in conclusion so.

But this is worshipful society,

And fits the mounting spirit like myself:

For he is but a bastard to the time,

That doth not smack of observation,—

And so am I, whether I smack or no;

And not alone in habit and device,

Exterior form, outward accoutrement,

But from the inward motion to deliver

Sweet, sweet, sweet poison for the age's tooth;

Which, though I will not practise to deceive,

Yet, to avoid deceit, I mean to learn;

For it shall strew the footsteps of my rising.—

But who comes in such haste in riding-robes?

What woman-post is this? hath she no husband

That will take pains to blow a horn before her?

[Enter LADY FALCONBRIDGE, and JAMES GURNEY.]

O me, 'tis my mother!—w now, good lady!

What brings you here to court so hastily?

LADY FALCONBRIDGE.

Where is that slave, thy brother? where is he

That holds in chase mine honour up and down?

BASTARD.

My brother Robert? old Sir Robert's son?

Colbrand the giant, that same mighty man?

Is it Sir Robert's son that you seek so?

LADY FalcoNBRIDGE.

Sir Robert's son! Ay, thou unreverend boy,

Sir Robert's son: why scorn'st thou at Sir Robert?

He is Sir Robert's son, and so art thou.

BASTARD.

James Gurney, wilt thou give us leave awhile?

GURNEY.

Good leave, good Philip.

BASTARD.

Philip—sparrow!—James,

There's toys abroad:—anon I'll tell thee more.

[Exit GURNEY.]

Madam, I was not old Sir Robert's son;

Sir Robert might have eat his part in me

Upon Good-Friday, and ne'er broke his fast.

Sir Robert could do well: marry, to confess,

Could not get me; Sir Robert could not do it,—

We know his handiwork:—therefore, good mother,

To whom am I beholding for these limbs?

Sir Robert never holp to make this leg.

LADY FALCONBRIDGE.

Hast thou conspired with thy brother too,

That for thine own gain shouldst defend mine honour?

What means this scorn, thou most untoward knave?

BASTARD.

Knight, knight, good mother,—Basilisco-like;

What! I am dubb'd; I have it on my shoulder.

But, mother, I am not Sir Robert's son:

I have disclaim'd Sir Robert and my land;

Legitimation, name, and all is gone:

Then, good my mother, let me know my father,—

Some proper man, I hope: who was it, mother?

LADY FalcoNBRIDGE.

Hast thou denied thyself a Falconbridge?

BASTARD.

As faithfully as I deny the devil.

LADY FALCONBRIDGE.

King Richard Coeur-de-lion was thy father:

By long and vehement suit I was seduc'd

To make room for him in my husband's bed:—

Heaven lay not my transgression to my charge!—

Thou art the issue of my dear offence,

Which was so strongly urg'd, past my defence.

BASTARD.

Now, by this light, were I to get again,

Madam, I would not wish a better father.

Some sins do bear their privilege on earth,

And so doth yours; your fault was not your folly:

Needs must you lay your heart at his dispose,—

Subjected tribute to commanding love,—

Against whose fury and unmatched force

The aweless lion could not wage the fight

Nor keep his princely heart from Richard's hand:

He that perforce robs lions of their hearts

May easily win a woman's. Ay, my mother,

With all my heart I thank thee for my father!

Who lives and dares but say, thou didst not well

When I was got, I'll send his soul to hell.

Come, lady, I will show thee to my kin;

And they shall say when Richard me begot,

If thou hadst said him nay, it had been sin:

Who says it was, he lies; I say 'twas not.

[Exeunt.]

ACT II.

SCENE 1. France. Before the walls of Angiers.

[Enter, on one side, the ARCHDUKE OF AUSTRIA and Forces; on the other, PHILIP, King of France, LOUIS, CONSTANCE, ARTHUR, and Forces.]

KING PHILIP.

Before Angiers well met, brave Austria.—

Arthur, that great forerunner of thy blood,

Richard, that robb'd the lion of his heart,

And fought the holy wars in Palestine,

By this brave duke came early to his grave:

And, for amends to his posterity,

At our importance hither is he come

To spread his colours, boy, in thy behalf;

And to rebuke the usurpation

Of thy unnatural uncle, English John:

Embrace him, love him, give him welcome hither.

ARTHUR.

God shall forgive you Coeur-de-lion's death

The rather that you give his offspring life,

Shadowing their right under your wings of war:

I give you welcome with a powerless hand,

But with a heart full of unstained love,—

Welcome before the gates of Angiers, duke.

LOUIS.

A noble boy! Who would not do thee right?

AUSTRIA.

Upon thy cheek lay I this zealous kiss,

As seal to this indenture of my love,—

That to my home I will no more return,

Till Angiers, and the right thou hast in France,

Together with that pale, that white-fac'd shore,

Whose foot spurns back the ocean's roaring tides,

And coops from other lands her islanders,—

Even till that England, hedg'd in with the main,

That water-walled bulwark, still secure

And confident from foreign purposes,—

Even till that utmost corner of the west

Salute thee for her king: till then, fair boy,

Will I not think of home, but follow arms.

CONSTANCE.

O, take his mother's thanks, a widow's thanks,

Till your strong hand shall help to give him strength

To make a more requital to your love!

AUSTRIA.

The peace of heaven is theirs that lift their swords

In such a just and charitable war.

KING PHILIP.

Well then, to work: our cannon shall be bent

Against the brows of this resisting town.—

Call for our chiefest men of discipline,

To cull the plots of best advantages:

We'll lay before this town our royal bones,

Wade to the market-place in Frenchmen's blood,

But we will make it subject to this boy.

CONSTANCE.

Stay for an answer to your embassy,

Lest unadvis'd you stain your swords with blood:

My Lord Chatillon may from England bring

That right in peace which here we urge in war;

And then we shall repent each drop of blood

That hot rash haste so indirectly shed.

KING PHILIP.

A wonder, lady!—lo, upon thy wish,

Our messenger Chatillon is arriv'd.

[Enter CHATILLON.]

What England says, say briefly, gentle lord;

We coldly pause for thee; Chatillon, speak.

CHATILLON.

Then turn your forces from this paltry siege,

And stir them up against a mightier task.

England, impatient of your just demands,

Hath put himself in arms: the adverse winds,

Whose leisure I have stay'd, have given him time

To land his legions all as soon as I;

His marches are expedient to this town,

His forces strong, his soldiers confident.

With him along is come the mother-queen,

An Ate, stirring him to blood and strife;

With her her neice, the Lady Blanch of Spain;

With them a bastard of the king's deceas'd:

And all the unsettled humours of the land,—

Rash, inconsiderate, fiery voluntaries,

With ladies' faces and fierce dragons' spleens,—

Have sold their fortunes at their native homes,

Bearing their birthrights proudly on their backs,

To make a hazard of new fortunes here.

In brief, a braver choice of dauntless spirits

Than now the English bottoms have waft o'er

Did never float upon the swelling tide

To do offence and scathe in Christendom.

[Drums beat within.]

The interruption of their churlish drums

Cuts off more circumstance: they are at hand;

To parley or to fight: therefore prepare.

KING PHILIP.

How much unlook'd-for is this expedition!

AUSTRIA.

By how much unexpected, by so much

We must awake endeavour for defence;

For courage mounteth with occasion:

Let them be welcome, then; we are prepar'd.

**[Enter KING JOHN, ELINOR, BLANCH, the BASTARD,
PEMBROKE, Lords, and Forces.]**

KING JOHN.

Peace be to France, if France in peace permit

Our just and lineal entrance to our own!

If not, bleed France, and peace ascend to heaven,

Whiles we, God's wrathful agent, do correct

Their proud contempt that beats his peace to heaven!

KING PHILIP.

Peace be to England, if that war return

From France to England, there to live in peace!

England we love; and for that England's sake

With burden of our armour here we sweat.

31

This toil of ours should be a work of thine;

But thou from loving England art so far

That thou hast under-wrought his lawful king,

Cut off the sequence of posterity,

Outfaced infant state, and done a rape

Upon the maiden virtue of the crown.

Look here upon thy brother Geffrey's face:—

These eyes, these brows, were moulded out of his:

This little abstract doth contain that large

Which died in Geffrey; and the hand of time

Shall draw this brief into as huge a volume.

That Geffrey was thy elder brother born,

And this his son; England was Geffrey's right,

And this is Geffrey's: in the name of God,

How comes it then, that thou art call'd a king,

When living blood doth in these temples beat,

Which owe the crown that thou o'er-masterest?

KING JOHN.

From whom hast thou this great commission, France,

To draw my answer from thy articles?

KING PHILIP.

From that supernal judge that stirs good thoughts

In any breast of strong authority,

To look into the blots and stains of right.

That judge hath made me guardian to this boy:

Under whose warrant I impeach thy wrong;

And by whose help I mean to chastise it.

KING JOHN.

Alack, thou dost usurp authority.

KING PHILIP.

Excus,—it is to beat usurping down.

ELINOR.

Who is it thou dost call usurper, France?

CONSTANCE.

Let me make answer;—thy usurping son.

ELINOR.

Out, insolent! thy bastard shall be king,

That thou mayst be a queen, and check the world!

CONSTANCE.

My bed was ever to thy son as true

As thine was to thy husband; and this boy

Liker in feature to his father Geffrey

Than thou and John in manners,—being as like

As rain to water, or devil to his dam.

My boy a bastard! By my soul, I think

His father never was so true begot:

It cannot be, an if thou wert his mother.

ELINOR.

There's a good mother, boy, that blots thy father.

CONSTANCE.

There's a good grandam, boy, that would blot thee.

AUSTRIA.

Peace!

BASTARD.

Hear the crier.

AUSTRIA.

What the devil art thou?

BASTARD.

One that will play the devil, sir, with you,

An 'a may catch your hide and you alone.

You are the hare of whom the proverb goes,

Whose valour plucks dead lions by the beard:

I'll smoke your skin-coat an I catch you right;

Sirrah, look to 't; i' faith I will, i' faith.

BLANCH.

O, well did he become that lion's robe

That did disrobe the lion of that robe!

BASTARD.

It lies as sightly on the back of him

As great Alcides' shows upon an ass:—

But, ass, I'll take that burden from your back,

Or lay on that shall make your shoulders crack.

AUSTRIA.

What cracker is this same that deafs our ears

With this abundance of superfluous breath?

KING PHILIP.

Louis, determine what we shall do straight.

LOUIS.

Women and fools, break off your conference.—

King John, this is the very sum of all,—

England and Ireland, Anjou, Touraine, Maine,

In right of Arthur, do I claim of thee:

Wilt thou resign them, and lay down thy arms?

KING JOHN.

My life as soon:—I do defy thee, France.

Arthur of Bretagne, yield thee to my hand;

And out of my dear love, I'll give thee more

Than e'er the coward hand of France can win:

Submit thee, boy.

ELINOR.

Come to thy grandam, child.

CONSTANCE.

Do, child, go to it' grandam, child;

Give grandam kingdom, and it' grandam will

Give it a plum, a cherry, and a fig.

There's a good grandam!

ARTHUR.

Good my mother, peace!

I would that I were low laid in my grave:

I am not worth this coil that's made for me.

ELINOR.

His mother shames him so, poor boy, he weeps.

CONSTANCE.

Now, shame upon you, whe'er she does or no!

His grandam's wrongs, and not his mother's shames,

Draws those heaven-moving pearls from his poor eyes,

Which heaven shall take in nature of a fee:

Ay, with these crystal beads heaven shall be brib'd

To do him justice, and revenge on you.

ELINOR.

Thou monstrous slanderer of heaven and earth!

CONSTANCE.

Thou monstrous injurer of heaven and earth!

Call not me slanderer: thou and thine usurp

The dominations, royalties, and rights,

Of this oppressed boy: this is thy eldest son's son,

Infortunate in nothing but in thee:

Thy sins are visited in this poor child;

The canon of the law is laid on him,

Being but the second generation

Removed from thy sin-conceiving womb.

KING JOHN.

Bedlam, have done.

CONSTANCE.

I have but this to say,—

That he is not only plagued for her sin,

But God hath made her sin and her the plague

On this removed issue, plagu'd for her

And with her plague, her sin; his injury

Her injury,—the beadle to her sin;

All punish'd in the person of this child,

And all for her: a plague upon her!

ELINOR.

Thou unadvised scold, I can produce

A will that bars the title of thy son.

CONSTANCE.

Ay, who doubts that? a will, a wicked will;

A woman's will; a canker'd grandam's will!

KING PHILIP.

Peace, lady! pause, or be more temperate:

It ill beseems this presence to cry aim

To these ill-tuned repetitions.—

Some trumpet summon hither to the walls

These men of Angiers: let us hear them speak

Whose title they admit, Arthur's or John's.

[Trumpet sounds. Enter citizens upon the walls.]

FIRST CITIZEN.

Who is it that hath warn'd us to the walls?

KING PHILIP.

'Tis France, for England.

KING JOHN.

England for itself:—

You men of Angiers, and my loving subjects,—

KING PHILIP.

You loving men of Angiers, Arthur's subjects,

Our trumpet call'd you to this gentle parle.

KING JOHN.

For our advantage; therefore hear us first.

These flags of France, that are advanced here

Before the eye and prospect of your town,

Have hither march'd to your endamagement;

The cannons have their bowels full of wrath,

And ready mounted are they to spit forth

Their iron indignation 'gainst your walls:

All preparation for a bloody siege

And merciless proceeding by these French

Confronts your city's eyes, your winking gates;

And, but for our approach, those sleeping stones

That as a waist doth girdle you about,

By the compulsion of their ordinance

By this time from their fixed beds of lime

Had been dishabited, and wide havoc made

For bloody power to rush upon your peace.

But, on the sight of us, your lawful king,—

Who, painfully, with much expedient march,

Have brought a countercheck before your gates,

To save unscratch'd your city's threatn'd cheeks,—

Behold, the French, amaz'd, vouchsafe a parle;

And now, instead of bullets wrapp'd in fire,

To make a shaking fever in your walls,

They shoot but calm words folded up in smoke,

To make a faithless error in your ears:

Which trust accordingly, kind citizens,

And let us in, your king; whose labour'd spirits,

Forwearied in this action of swift speed,

Craves harbourage within your city-walls.

KING PHILIP.

When I have said, make answer to us both.

Lo, in this right hand, whose protection

Is most divinely vow'd upon the right

Of him it holds, stands young Plantagenet,

Son to the elder brother of this man,

And king o'er him and all that he enjoys:

For this down-trodden equity we tread

In war-like march these greens before your town;

Being no further enemy to you

Than the constraint of hospitable zeal

In the relief of this oppressed child

Religiously provokes. Be pleased then

To pay that duty which you truly owe

To him that owes it, namely, this young prince:

And then our arms, like to a muzzled bear,

Save in aspect, hath all offence seal'd up;

Our cannons' malice vainly shall be spent

Against the invulnerable clouds of heaven;

And with a blessed and unvex'd retire,

With unhack'd swords and helmets all unbruis'd,

We will bear home that lusty blood again

Which here we came to spout against your town,

And leave your children, wives, and you, in peace.

But if you fondly pass our proffer'd offer,

'Tis not the roundure of your old-fac'd walls

Can hide you from our messengers of war,

Though all these English, and their discipline,

Were harbour'd in their rude circumference.

Then, tell us, shall your city call us lord

In that behalf which we have challeng'd it?

Or shall we give the signal to our rage,

And stalk in blood to our possession?

FIRST CITIZEN.

In brief: we are the King of England's subjects:

For him, and in his right, we hold this town.

KING JOHN.

Acknowledge then the king, and let me in.

CITIZEN.

That can we not; but he that proves the king,

To him will we prove loyal: till that time

Have we ramm'd up our gates against the world.

KING JOHN.

Doth not the crown of England prove the king?

And if not that, I bring you witnesses,

Twice fifteen thousand hearts of England's breed,—

KING JOHN.

BASTARD.

Bastards, and else.

KING JOHN.

To verify our title with their lives.

KING PHILIP.

As many and as well-born bloods as those,—

BASTARD.

Some bastards too.

KING PHILIP.

Stand in his face, to contradict his claim.

FIRST CITIZEN.

Till you compound whose right is worthiest,

We for the worthiest hold the right from both.

KING JOHN.

Then God forgive the sin of all those souls

That to their everlasting residence,

Before the dew of evening fall, shall fleet,

In dreadful trial of our kingdom's king!

KING PHILIP.

Amen, Amen!—Mount, chevaliers; to arms!

BASTARD.

Saint George, that swinged the dragon, and e'er since

Sits on his horse' back at mine hostess' door,

Teach us some fence!—Sirrah [To AUSTRIA.], were I at home,

At your den, sirrah, with your lioness,

I would set an ox-head to your lion's hide,

And make a monster of you.

AUSTRIA.

Peace! no more.

BASTARD.

O, tremble, for you hear the lion roar.

KING JOHN.

Up higher to the plain; where we'll set forth

In best appointment all our regiments.

BASTARD.

Speed, then, to take advantage of the field.

KING PHILIP.

It shall be so;—[To LOUIS.] and at the other hill

Command the rest to stand.—God and our right!

[Exeunt severally.]

[After excursions, enter a French Herald, with trumpets, to the gates.]

FRENCH HERALD.

You men of Angiers, open wide your gates

And let young Arthur, Duke of Bretagne, in,

Who, by the hand of France, this day hath made

Much work for tears in many an English mother,

Whose sons lie scatter'd on the bleeding ground;

Many a widow's husband grovelling lies,

Coldly embracing the discolour'd earth;

And victory, with little loss, doth play

Upon the dancing banners of the French,

Who are at hand, triumphantly display'd,

To enter conquerors, and to proclaim

Arthur of Bretagne England's king and yours.

[Enter an ENGLISH HERALD, with trumpets.]

ENGLISH HERALD.

Rejoice, you men of Angiers, ring your bells:

King John, your king and England's, doth approach,

Commander of this hot malicious day:

Their armours, that march'd hence so silver-bright,

Hither return all gilt with Frenchmen's blood;

There stuck no plume in any English crest

That is removed by a staff of France,

Our colours do return in those same hands

That did display them when we first march'd forth;

And, like a jolly troop of huntsmen, come

Our lusty English, all with purpled hands,

Dy'd in the dying slaughter of their foes:

Open your gates and give the victors way.

FIRST CITIZEN.

Heralds, from off our towers, we might behold,

From first to last, the onset and retire

Of both your armies; whose equality

By our best eyes cannot be censured:

Blood hath bought blood, and blows have answer'd blows;

Strength match'd with strength, and power confronted power:

Both are alike, and both alike we like.

One must prove greatest: while they weigh so even,

We hold our town for neither; yet for both.

[Enter, on one side, KING JOHN, ELINOR, BLANCH, the BASTARD, and Forces; at the other, KING PHILIP, LOUIS, AUSTRIA, and Forces.]

KING JOHN.

France, hast thou yet more blood to cast away?

Say, shall the current of our right run on?

Whose passage, vex'd with thy impediment,

Shall leave his native channel, and o'erswell

With course disturb'd even thy confining shores,

Unless thou let his silver water keep

A peaceful progress to the ocean.

KING PHILIP.

England, thou hast not sav'd one drop of blood

In this hot trial, more than we of France;

Rather, lost more: and by this hand I swear,

That sways the earth this climate overlooks,

Before we will lay down our just-borne arms,

We'll put thee down, 'gainst whom these arms we bear,

Or add a royal number to the dead,

Gracing the scroll that tells of this war's loss

With slaughter coupled to the name of kings.

BASTARD.

Ha, majesty! how high thy glory towers

When the rich blood of kings is set on fire!

O, now doth Death line his dead chaps with steel;

The swords of soldiers are his teeth, his fangs;

And now he feasts, mousing the flesh of men,

In undetermin'd differences of kings.—

Why stand these royal fronts amazed thus?

Cry, havoc, kings! back to the stained field,

You equal potents, fiery-kindled spirits!

Then let confusion of one part confirm

The other's peace: till then, blows, blood, and death!

KING JOHN.

Whose party do the townsmen yet admit?

KING PHILIP.

Speak, citizens, for England; who's your king?

FIRST CITIZEN.

The King of England, when we know the king.

KING PHILIP.

Know him in us, that here hold up his right.

KING JOHN.

In us, that are our own great deputy,

And bear possession of our person here;

Lord of our presence, Angiers, and of you.

FIRST CITIZEN.

A greater power than we denies all this;

And till it be undoubted, we do lock

Our former scruple in our strong-barr'd gates;

King'd of our fears, until our fears, resolv'd,

Be by some certain king purg'd and depos'd.

BASTARD.

By heaven, these scroyles of Angiers flout you, kings,

And stand securely on their battlements

As in a theatre, whence they gape and point

At your industrious scenes and acts of death.

Your royal presences be rul'd by me:—

Do like the mutines of Jerusalem,

Be friends awhile, and both conjointly bend

Your sharpest deeds of malice on this town:

By east and west let France and England mount

Their battering cannon, charged to the mouths,

Till their soul-fearing clamours have brawl'd down

The flinty ribs of this contemptuous city:

I'd play incessantly upon these jades,

Even till unfenced desolation

Leave them as naked as the vulgar air.

That done, dissever your united strengths,

And part your mingled colours once again:

Turn face to face, and bloody point to point;

Then, in a moment, fortune shall cull forth

Out of one side her happy minion,

To whom in favour she shall give the day,

And kiss him with a glorious victory.

How like you this wild counsel, mighty states?

Smacks it not something of the policy?

KING JOHN.

Now, by the sky that hangs above our heads,

I like it well.—France, shall we knit our powers,

And lay this Angiers even with the ground;

Then, after, fight who shall be king of it?

BASTARD.

An if thou hast the mettle of a king,—

Being wrong'd, as we are, by this peevish town,—

Turn thou the mouth of thy artillery,

As we will ours, against these saucy walls;

And when that we have dash'd them to the ground,

Why then defy each other, and, pell-mell,

Make work upon ourselves, for heaven or hell!

KING PHILIP.

Let it be so.—Say, where will you assault?

KING JOHN.

We from the west will send destruction

Into this city's bosom.

AUSTRIA.

I from the north.

KING PHILIP.

Our thunder from the south

Shall rain their drift of bullets on this town.

BASTARD.

O prudent discipline! From north to south,—

Austria and France shoot in each other's mouth:

I'll stir them to it.[Aside.]—Come, away, away!

FIRST CITIZEN.

Hear us, great kings: vouchsafe awhile to stay,

And I shall show you peace and fair-fac'd league;

Win you this city without stroke or wound;

Rescue those breathing lives to die in beds

That here come sacrifices for the field:

Persever not, but hear me, mighty kings.

KING JOHN.

Speak on with favour; we are bent to hear.

FIRST CITIZEN.

That daughter there of Spain, the Lady Blanch,

Is niece to England:—look upon the years

Of Louis the Dauphin and that lovely maid:

If lusty love should go in quest of beauty,

Where should he find it fairer than in Blanch?

If zealous love should go in search of virtue,

Where should he find it purer than in Blanch?

If love ambitious sought a match of birth,

Whose veins bound richer blood than Lady Blanch?

Such as she is, in beauty, virtue, birth,

Is the young Dauphin every way complete,—

If not complete of, say he is not she;

And she again wants nothing, to name want,

If want it be not, that she is not he:

He is the half part of a blessed man,

Left to be finished by such a she;

And she a fair divided excellence,

Whose fulness of perfection lies in him.

O, two such silver currents, when they join

Do glorify the banks that bound them in;

And two such shores to two such streams made one,

Two such controlling bounds, shall you be, kings,

To these two princes, if you marry them.

This union shall do more than battery can

To our fast-closed gates; for at this match,

With swifter spleen than powder can enforce,

The mouth of passage shall we fling wide ope,

And give you entrance; but without this match,

The sea enraged is not half so deaf,

Lions more confident, mountains and rocks

More free from motion; no, not Death himself

In mortal fury half so peremptory

As we to keep this city.

BASTARD.

Here's a stay

That shakes the rotten carcase of old Death

Out of his rags! Here's a large mouth, indeed,

That spits forth death and mountains, rocks and seas;

Talks as familiarly of roaring lions

As maids of thirteen do of puppy-dogs!

What cannoneer begot this lusty blood?

He speaks plain cannon,—fire and smoke and bounce;

He gives the bastinado with his tongue;

Our ears are cudgell'd; not a word of his

But buffets better than a fist of France.

Zounds! I was never so bethump'd with words

Since I first call'd my brother's father dad.

ELINOR.

Son, list to this conjunction, make this match;

Give with our niece a dowry large enough;

For by this knot thou shalt so surely tie

Thy now unsur'd assurance to the crown,

That yon green boy shall have no sun to ripe

The bloom that promiseth a mighty fruit.

I see a yielding in the looks of France;

Mark how they whisper: urge them while their souls

Are capable of this ambition,

Lest zeal, now melted by the windy breath

Of soft petitions, pity, and remorse,

Cool and congeal again to what it was.

FIRST CITIZEN.

Why answer not the double majesties

This friendly treaty of our threaten'd town?

KING PHILIP.

Speak England first, that hath been forward first

To speak unto this city: what say you?

KING JOHN.

If that the Dauphin there, thy princely son,

Can in this book of beauty read 'I love,'

Her dowry shall weigh equal with a queen;

For Anjou, and fair Touraine, Maine, Poictiers,

And all that we upon this side the sea,—

Except this city now by us besieg'd,—

Find liable to our crown and dignity,

Shall gild her bridal bed; and make her rich

In titles, honours, and promotions,

As she in beauty, education, blood,

Holds hand with any princess of the world.

KING PHILIP.

What say'st thou, boy? look in the lady's face.

LOUIS.

I do, my lord, and in her eye I find

A wonder, or a wondrous miracle,

The shadow of myself form'd in her eye;

Which, being but the shadow of your son,

Becomes a sun, and makes your son a shadow:

I do protest I never lov'd myself

Till now infixed I beheld myself

Drawn in the flattering table of her eye.

[Whispers with BLANCH.]

BASTARD.

[Aside.] Drawn in the flattering table of her eye!—

Hang'd in the frowning wrinkle of her brow,

And quarter'd in her heart!—he doth espy

Himself love's traitor! This is pity now,

That, hang'd, and drawn, and quarter'd, there should be

In such a love so vile a lout as he.

BLANCH.

My uncle's will in this respect is mine.

If he see aught in you that makes him like,

That anything he sees, which moves his liking

I can with ease translate it to my will;

Or if you will, to speak more properly,

I will enforce it easily to my love.

Further, I will not flatter you, my lord,

That all I see in you is worthy love,

Than this,—that nothing do I see in you,

Though churlish thoughts themselves should be your judge,—

That I can find should merit any hate.

KING JOHN.

What say these young ones?—What say you, my niece?

BLANCH.

That she is bound in honour still to do

What you in wisdom still vouchsafe to say.

KING JOHN.

Speak then, Prince Dauphin; can you love this lady?

LOUIS.

Nay, ask me if I can refrain from love;

For I do love her most unfeignedly.

KING JOHN.

Then do I give Volquessen, Touraine, Maine,

Poictiers, and Anjou, these five provinces,

With her to thee; and this addition more,

Full thirty thousand marks of English coin.—

Philip of France, if thou be pleas'd withal,

Command thy son and daughter to join hands.

KING PHILIP.

It likes us well.—Young princes, close your hands.

AUSTRIA.

And your lips too; for I am well assur'd

That I did so when I was first assur'd.

KING PHILIP.

Now, citizens of Angiers, ope your gates,

Let in that amity which you have made;

For at Saint Mary's chapel presently

The rites of marriage shall be solemniz'd.—

Is not the Lady Constance in this troop?

I know she is not; for this match made up

Her presence would have interrupted much:

Where is she and her son? tell me, who knows.

LOUIS.

She is sad and passionate at your highness' tent.

KING PHILIP.

And, by my faith, this league that we have made

Will give her sadness very little cure.—

Brother of England, how may we content

This widow lady? In her right we came;

Which we, God knows, have turn'd another way,

To our own vantage.

KING JOHN.

We will heal up all;

For we'll create young Arthur Duke of Bretagne,

And Earl of Richmond; and this rich fair town

We make him lord of.—Call the Lady Constance:

Some speedy messenger bid her repair

To our solemnity:—I trust we shall,

If not fill up the measure of her will,

Yet in some measure satisfy her so

That we shall stop her exclamation.

Go we, as well as haste will suffer us,

To this unlook'd-for, unprepared pomp.

    [Exeunt all but the BASTARD. The Citizens retire from the Walls.]

BASTARD.

Mad world! mad kings! mad composition!

John, to stop Arthur's title in the whole,

Hath willingly departed with a part;

And France,—whose armour conscience buckled on,

Whom zeal and charity brought to the field

As God's own soldier,—rounded in the ear

With that same purpose-changer, that sly devil;

That broker, that still breaks the pate of faith;

That daily break-vow, he that wins of all,

Of kings, of beggars, old men, young men, maids,—

Who having no external thing to lose

But the word maid, cheats the poor maid of that;

That smooth-fac'd gentleman, tickling commodity,—

Commodity, the bias of the world;

The world, who of itself is peised well,

Made to run even upon even ground,

Till this advantage, this vile-drawing bias,

This sway of motion, this commodity,

Makes it take head from all indifferency,

From all direction, purpose, course, intent:

And this same bias, this commodity,

This bawd, this broker, this all-changing word,

Clapp'd on the outward eye of fickle France,

Hath drawn him from his own determin'd aid,

From a resolv'd and honourable war,

To a most base and vile-concluded peace.—

And why rail I on this commodity?

But for because he hath not woo'd me yet:

Not that I have the power to clutch my hand

When his fair angels would salute my palm;

But for my hand, as unattempted yet,

Like a poor beggar, raileth on the rich.

Well, whiles I am a beggar, I will rail,

And say, There is no sin but to be rich;

And being rich, my virtue then shall be,

To say, There is no vice but beggary:

Since kings break faith upon commodity,

Gain, be my lord!—for I will worship thee.

[Exit.]

ACT III.

SCENE 1. France. The FRENCH KING'S tent.

[Enter CONSTANCE, ARTHUR, and SALISBURY.]

CONSTANCE.

Gone to be married! gone to swear a peace!

False blood to false blood join'd! gone to be friends!

Shall Louis have Blanch? and Blanch those provinces?

It is not so; thou hast misspoke, misheard;

Be well advis'd, tell o'er thy tale again:

It cannot be; thou dost but say 'tis so;

I trust I may not trust thee; for thy word

Is but the vain breath of a common man:

Believe me, I do not believe thee, man;

I have a king's oath to the contrary.

Thou shalt be punish'd for thus frighting me,

For I am sick and capable of fears;

Oppress'd with wrongs, and therefore full of fears;

A widow, husbandless, subject to fears;

A woman, naturally born to fears;

And though thou now confess thou didst but jest,

With my vex'd spirits I cannot take a truce,

But they will quake and tremble all this day.

What dost thou mean by shaking of thy head?

Why dost thou look so sadly on my son?

What means that hand upon that breast of thine?

Why holds thine eye that lamentable rheum,

Like a proud river peering o'er his bounds?

Be these sad signs confirmers of thy words?

Then speak again,—not all thy former tale,

But this one word, whether thy tale be true.

SALISBURY.

As true as I believe you think them false

That give you cause to prove my saying true.

CONSTANCE.

O, if thou teach me to believe this sorrow,

Teach thou this sorrow how to make me die;

And let belief and life encounter so

As doth the fury of two desperate men,

Which in the very meeting fall and die!—

Louis marry Blanch! O boy, then where art thou?

France friend with England! what becomes of me?—

Fellow, be gone: I cannot brook thy sight;

This news hath made thee a most ugly man.

SALISBURY.

What other harm have I, good lady, done,

But spoke the harm that is by others done?

CONSTANCE.

Which harm within itself so heinous is,

As it makes harmful all that speak of it.

ARTHUR.

I do beseech you, madam, be content.

CONSTANCE.

If thou, that bid'st me be content, wert grim,

Ugly, and slanderous to thy mother's womb,

Full of unpleasing blots and sightless stains,

Lame, foolish, crooked, swart, prodigious,

Patch'd with foul moles and eye-offending marks,

I would not care, I then would be content;

For then I should not love thee; no, nor thou

Become thy great birth, nor deserve a crown.

But thou art fair; and at thy birth, dear boy,

Nature and fortune join'd to make thee great:

Of nature's gifts thou mayst with lilies boast,

And with the half-blown rose; but Fortune, O!

She is corrupted, chang'd, and won from thee;

She adulterates hourly with thine uncle John;

And with her golden hand hath pluck'd on France

To tread down fair respect of sovereignty,

And made his majesty the bawd to theirs.

France is a bawd to Fortune and king John—

That strumpet Fortune, that usurping John!—

Tell me, thou fellow, is not France forsworn?

Envenom him with words; or get thee gone,

And leave those woes alone, which I alone

Am bound to under-bear.

SALISBURY.

Pardon me, madam,

I may not go without you to the kings.

CONSTANCE.

Thou mayst, thou shalt; I will not go with thee:

I will instruct my sorrows to be proud;

For grief is proud, and makes his owner stout.

To me, and to the state of my great grief,

Let kings assemble; for my grief's so great

That no supporter but the huge firm earth

Can hold it up: here I and sorrows sit;

Here is my throne, bid kings come bow to it.

[Seats herself on the ground.]

**[Enter KING JOHN, KING PHILIP, LOUIS, BLANCH, ELINOR,
BASTARD, AUSTRIA, and attendants.]**

KING PHILIP.

'Tis true, fair daughter; and this blessed day

Ever in France shall be kept festival:

To solemnize this day the glorious sun

Stays in his course and plays the alchemist,

Turning, with splendour of his precious eye,

The meagre cloddy earth to glittering gold:

The yearly course that brings this day about

Shall never see it but a holiday.

CONSTANCE.

[Rising.] A wicked day, and not a holy day!

What hath this day deserv'd? what hath it done

That it in golden letters should be set

Among the high tides in the calendar?

Nay, rather turn this day out of the week,

This day of shame, oppression, perjury:

Or, if it must stand still, let wives with child

Pray that their burdens may not fall this day,

Lest that their hopes prodigiously be cross'd:

But on this day let seamen fear no wreck;

No bargains break that are not this day made:

This day, all things begun come to ill end,—

Yea, faith itself to hollow falsehood change!

KING PHILIP.

By heaven, lady, you shall have no cause

To curse the fair proceedings of this day.

Have I not pawn'd to you my majesty?

CONSTANCE.

You have beguil'd me with a counterfeit

Resembling majesty; which, being touch'd and tried,

Proves valueless; you are forsworn, forsworn:

You came in arms to spill mine enemies' blood,

But now in arms you strengthen it with yours:

The grappling vigour and rough frown of war

Is cold in amity and painted peace,

And our oppression hath made up this league.—

Arm, arm, you heavens, against these perjur'd kings!

A widow cries: be husband to me, heavens!

Let not the hours of this ungodly day

Wear out the day in peace; but, ere sunset,

Set armed discord 'twixt these perjur'd kings!

Hear me, O, hear me!

AUSTRIA.

Lady Constance, peace!

CONSTANCE.

War! war! no peace! peace is to me a war.

O Lymoges! O Austria! thou dost shame

That bloody spoil: thou slave, thou wretch, thou coward!

Thou little valiant, great in villainy!

Thou ever strong upon the stronger side!

Thou Fortune's champion that dost never fight

But when her humorous ladyship is by

To teach thee safety!—thou art perjur'd too,

And sooth'st up greatness. What a fool art thou,

A ramping fool, to brag, and stamp. and swear

Upon my party! Thou cold-blooded slave,

Hast thou not spoke like thunder on my side?

Been sworn my soldier? bidding me depend

Upon thy stars, thy fortune, and thy strength?

And dost thou now fall over to my foes?

Thou wear a lion's hide! doff it for shame,

And hang a calf's-skin on those recreant limbs!

AUSTRIA.

O that a man should speak those words to me!

BASTARD.

And hang a calf's-skin on those recreant limbs.

AUSTRIA.

Thou dar'st not say so, villain, for thy life.

BASTARD.

And hang a calf's-skin on those recreant limbs.

KING JOHN.

We like not this: thou dost forget thyself.

KING PHILIP.

Here comes the holy legate of the Pope.

[Enter PANDULPH.]

PANDULPH.

Hail, you anointed deputies of heaven!—

To thee, King John, my holy errand is.

I Pandulph, of fair Milan cardinal,

And from Pope Innocent the legate here,

Do in his name religiously demand

Why thou against the church, our holy mother,

So wilfully dost spurn; and, force perforce

Keep Stephen Langton, chosen Archbishop

Of Canterbury, from that holy see?

This, in our foresaid holy father's name,

Pope Innocent, I do demand of thee.

KING JOHN.

What earthly name to interrogatories

Can task the free breath of a sacred king?

Thou canst not, cardinal, devise a name

So slight, unworthy, and ridiculous,

To charge me to an answer, as the pope.

Tell him this tale; and from the mouth of England

Add thus much more,—that no Italian priest

Shall tithe or toll in our dominions:

But as we under heaven are supreme head,

So, under him, that great supremacy,

Where we do reign, we will alone uphold,

Without the assistance of a mortal hand:

So tell the pope, all reverence set apart

To him and his usurp'd authority.

KING PHILIP.

Brother of England, you blaspheme in this.

KING JOHN.

Though you and all the kings of Christendom

Are led so grossly by this meddling priest,

Dreading the curse that money may buy out;

And by the merit of vile gold, dross, dust,

Purchase corrupted pardon of a man,

Who in that sale sells pardon from himself;

Though you and all the rest, so grossly led,

This juggling witchcraft with revenue cherish;

Yet I, alone, alone do me oppose

Against the pope, and count his friends my foes.

PANDULPH.

Then by the lawful power that I have,

Thou shalt stand curs'd and excommunicate:

And blessed shall he be that doth revolt

From his allegiance to an heretic;

And meritorious shall that hand be call'd,

Canonized, and worshipp'd as a saint,

That takes away by any secret course

Thy hateful life.

CONSTANCE.

O, lawful let it be

That I have room with Rome to curse awhile!

Good father Cardinal, cry thou amen

To my keen curses: for without my wrong

There is no tongue hath power to curse him right.

PANDULPH.

There's law and warrant, lady, for my curse.

CONSTANCE.

And for mine too: when law can do no right,

Let it be lawful that law bar no wrong:

Law cannot give my child his kingdom here;

For he that holds his kingdom holds the law:

Therefore, since law itself is perfect wrong,

How can the law forbid my tongue to curse?

PANDULPH.

Philip of France, on peril of a curse,

Let go the hand of that arch-heretic,

And raise the power of France upon his head,

Unless he do submit himself to Rome.

ELINOR.

Look'st thou pale, France; do not let go thy hand.

CONSTANCE

Look to that, devil; lest that France repent

And, by disjoining hands, hell lose a soul.

AUSTRIA.

King Philip, listen to the cardinal.

BASTARD.

And hang a calf's-skin on his recreant limbs.

AUSTRIA.

Well, ruffian, I must pocket up these wrongs,

Because—

BASTARD.

Your breeches best may carry them.

KING JOHN.

Philip, what say'st thou to the cardinal?

CONSTANCE.

What should he say, but as the cardinal?

LOUIS.

Bethink you, father; for the difference

Is, purchase of a heavy curse from Rome,

Or the light loss of England for a friend:

Forgo the easier.

BLANCH.

That's the curse of Rome.

CONSTANCE.

O Louis, stand fast! The devil tempts thee here

In likeness of a new uptrimmed bride.

BLANCH.

The Lady Constance speaks not from her faith,

But from her need.

CONSTANCE.

O, if thou grant my need,

Which only lives but by the death of faith,

That need must needs infer this principle,—

That faith would live again by death of need!

O then, tread down my need, and faith mounts up;

Keep my need up, and faith is trodden down!

KING JOHN.

The king is mov'd, and answers not to this.

CONSTANCE.

O be remov'd from him, and answer well!

AUSTRIA.

Do so, King Philip; hang no more in doubt.

BASTARD.

Hang nothing but a calf's-skin, most sweet lout.

KING PHILIP.

I am perplex'd, and know not what to say.

PANDULPH.

What canst thou say, but will perplex thee more,

If thou stand excommunicate and curs'd?

KING PHILIP.

Good reverend father, make my person yours,

And tell me how you would bestow yourself.

This royal hand and mine are newly knit,

And the conjunction of our inward souls

Married in league, coupled and link'd together

With all religious strength of sacred vows;

The latest breath that gave the sound of words

Was deep-sworn faith, peace, amity, true love,

Between our kingdoms and our royal selves;

And even before this truce, but new before,—

No longer than we well could wash our hands,

To clap this royal bargain up of peace,—

Heaven knows, they were besmear'd and overstain'd

With slaughter's pencil, where revenge did paint

The fearful difference of incensed kings:

And shall these hands, so lately purg'd of blood,

So newly join'd in love, so strong in both,

Unyoke this seizure and this kind regreet?

Play fast and loose with faith? so jest with heaven,

Make such unconstant children of ourselves,

As now again to snatch our palm from palm;

Unswear faith sworn; and on the marriage-bed

Of smiling peace to march a bloody host,

And make a riot on the gentle brow

Of true sincerity? O, holy sir.

My reverend father, let it not be so!

Out of your grace, devise, ordain, impose,

Some gentle order; and then we shall be bless'd

To do your pleasure, and continue friends.

PANDULPH.

All form is formless, order orderless,

Save what is opposite to England's love.

Therefore, to arms! be champion of our church,

Or let the church, our mother, breathe her curse,—

A mother's curse,—on her revolting son.

France, thou mayst hold a serpent by the tongue,

A chafed lion by the mortal paw,

A fasting tiger safer by the tooth,

Than keep in peace that hand which thou dost hold.

KING PHILIP.

I may disjoin my hand, but not my faith.

PANDULPH.

So mak'st thou faith an enemy to faith;

And, like a civil war, sett'st oath to oath,

Thy tongue against thy tongue. O, let thy vow

First made to heaven, first be to heaven perform'd,—

That is, to be the champion of our church.

What since thou swor'st is sworn against thyself

And may not be performed by thyself:

For that which thou hast sworn to do amiss

Is not amiss when it is truly done;

And being not done, where doing tends to ill,

The truth is then most done not doing it:

The better act of purposes mistook

Is to mistake again; though indirect,

Yet indirection thereby grows direct,

And falsehood falsehood cures, as fire cools fire

Within the scorched veins of one new-burn'd.

It is religion that doth make vows kept;

But thou hast sworn against religion,

By what thou swear'st against the thing thou swear'st;

And mak'st an oath the surety for thy truth

Against an oath: the truth thou art unsure

To swear, swears only not to be forsworn;

Else what a mockery should it be to swear!

But thou dost swear only to be forsworn;

And most forsworn, to keep what thou dost swear.

Therefore thy latter vows against thy first

Is in thyself rebellion to thyself;

And better conquest never canst thou make

Than arm thy constant and thy nobler parts

Against these giddy loose suggestions:

Upon which better part our prayers come in,

If thou vouchsafe them; but if not, then know

The peril of our curses fight on thee,

So heavy as thou shalt not shake them off,

But in despair die under the black weight.

AUSTRIA.

Rebellion, flat rebellion!

BASTARD.

Will't not be?

Will not a calf's-skin stop that mouth of thine?

LOUIS.

Father, to arms!

BLANCH.

Upon thy wedding-day?

Against the blood that thou hast married?

What, shall our feast be kept with slaughter'd men?

Shall braying trumpets and loud churlish drums,—

Clamours of hell,—be measures to our pomp?

O husband, hear me!—ay, alack, how new

Is husband in my mouth!—even for that name,

Which till this time my tongue did ne'er pronounce,

Upon my knee I beg, go not to arms

Against mine uncle.

CONSTANCE.

O, upon my knee,

Made hard with kneeling, I do pray to thee,

Thou virtuous Dauphin, alter not the doom

Forethought by heaven.

BLANCH.

Now shall I see thy love: what motive may

Be stronger with thee than the name of wife?

CONSTANCE.

That which upholdeth him that thee upholds,

His honour:—O, thine honour, Louis, thine honour!

LOUIS.

I muse your majesty doth seem so cold,

When such profound respects do pull you on.

PANDULPH.

I will denounce a curse upon his head.

KING PHILIP.

Thou shalt not need.—England, I will fall from thee.

CONSTANCE.

O fair return of banish'd majesty!

ELINOR.

O foul revolt of French inconstancy!

KING JOHN.

France, thou shalt rue this hour within this hour.

BASTARD.

Old Time the clock-setter, that bald sexton Time,

Is it as he will? well, then, France shall rue.

BLANCH.

The sun's o'ercast with blood: fair day, adieu!

Which is the side that I must go withal?

I am with both: each army hath a hand;

And in their rage, I having hold of both,

They whirl asunder and dismember me.

Husband, I cannot pray that thou mayst win;

Uncle, I needs must pray that thou mayst lose;

Father, I may not wish the fortune thine;

Grandam, I will not wish thy wishes thrive:

Whoever wins, on that side shall I lose;

Assured loss before the match be play'd.

LOUIS.

Lady, with me: with me thy fortune lies.

BLANCH.

There where my fortune lives, there my life dies.

KING JOHN.

Cousin, go draw our puissance together.—

[Exit BASTARD.]

France, I am burn'd up with inflaming wrath;

A rage whose heat hath this condition,

That nothing can allay, nothing but blood,—

The blood, and dearest-valu'd blood of France.

KING PHILIP.

Thy rage shall burn thee up, and thou shalt turn

To ashes, ere our blood shall quench that fire:

Look to thyself, thou art in jeopardy.

KING JOHN.

No more than he that threats.—To arms let's hie!

[Exeunt severally.]

SCENE 2. The same. Plains near Angiers

[Alarums. Excursions. Enter the BASTARD with AUSTRIA'S head.]

BASTARD.

Now, by my life, this day grows wondrous hot;

Some airy devil hovers in the sky

And pours down mischief.—Austria's head lie there,

While Philip breathes.

[Enter KING JOHN, ARTHUR, and HUBERT.]

KING JOHN.

Hubert, keep this boy.—Philip, make up:

My mother is assailed in our tent,

And ta'en, I fear.

BASTARD.

My lord, I rescu'd her;

Her highness is in safety, fear you not:

But on, my liege; for very little pains

Will bring this labour to an happy end.

[Exeunt.]

SCENE 3. The same.

[Alarums, Excursions, Retreat. Enter KING JOHN, ELINOR, ARTHUR, the BASTARD, HUBERT, and LORDS.]

KING JOHN.

[To ELINOR] So shall it be; your grace shall stay behind,

So strongly guarded.—

[To ARTHUR] Cousin, look not sad;

Thy grandam loves thee, and thy uncle will

As dear be to thee as thy father was.

ARTHUR.

O, this will make my mother die with grief!

KING JOHN.

Cousin [To the BASTARD], away for England; haste before:

And, ere our coming, see thou shake the bags

Of hoarding abbots; imprison'd angels

Set at liberty: the fat ribs of peace

Must by the hungry now be fed upon:

Use our commission in his utmost force.

BASTARD.

Bell, book, and candle shall not drive me back,

When gold and silver becks me to come on.

I leave your highness.—Grandam, I will pray,—

If ever I remember to be holy,—

For your fair safety; so, I kiss your hand.

ELINOR.

Farewell, gentle cousin.

KING JOHN.

Coz, farewell.

[Exit BASTARD.]

ELINOR.

Come hither, little kinsman; hark, a word.

[She takes Arthur aside.]

KING JOHN.

Come hither, Hubert. O my gentle Hubert,

We owe thee much! within this wall of flesh

There is a soul counts thee her creditor,

And with advantage means to pay thy love:

And, my good friend, thy voluntary oath

Lives in this bosom, dearly cherished.

Give me thy hand. I had a thing to say,—

But I will fit it with some better time.

By heaven, Hubert, I am almost asham'd

To say what good respect I have of thee.

HUBERT.

I am much bounden to your majesty.

KING JOHN.

80

Good friend, thou hast no cause to say so yet:

But thou shalt have; and creep time ne'er so slow,

Yet it shall come for me to do thee good.

I had a thing to say,—but let it go:

The sun is in the heaven, and the proud day,

Attended with the pleasures of the world,

Is all too wanton and too full of gawds

To give me audience:—if the midnight bell

Did, with his iron tongue and brazen mouth,

Sound on into the drowsy race of night;

If this same were a churchyard where we stand,

And thou possessed with a thousand wrongs;

Or if that surly spirit, melancholy,

Had bak'd thy blood and made it heavy-thick,

Which else runs tickling up and down the veins,

Making that idiot, laughter, keep men's eyes,

And strain their cheeks to idle merriment—

A passion hateful to my purposes;—

Or if that thou couldst see me without eyes,

Hear me without thine ears, and make reply

Without a tongue, using conceit alone,

Without eyes, ears, and harmful sound of words,—

Then, in despite of brooded watchful day,

I would into thy bosom pour my thoughts:

But, ah, I will not!—yet I love thee well;

And, by my troth, I think thou lov'st me well.

HUBERT.

So well that what you bid me undertake,

Though that my death were adjunct to my act,

By heaven, I would do it.

KING JOHN.

Do not I know thou wouldst?

Good Hubert, Hubert, Hubert, throw thine eye

On yon young boy: I'll tell thee what, my friend,

He is a very serpent in my way;

And wheresoe'er this foot of mine doth tread,

He lies before me: dost thou understand me?

Thou art his keeper.

HUBERT.

And I'll keep him so

That he shall not offend your majesty.

KING JOHN.

Death.

HUBERT.

My lord?

KING JOHN.

A grave.

HUBERT.

He shall not live.

KING JOHN.

Enough!—

I could be merry now. Hubert, I love thee;

Well, I'll not say what I intend for thee:

Remember.—Madam, fare you well:

I'll send those powers o'er to your majesty.

ELINOR.

My blessing go with thee!

KING JOHN.

For England, cousin, go:

Hubert shall be your man, attend on you

With all true duty.—On toward Calais, ho!

[Exeunt.]

SCENE 4. The same. The FRENCH KING's tent.

[Enter KING PHILIP, LOUIS, PANDULPH, and Attendants.]

KING PHILIP.

So, by a roaring tempest on the flood

A whole armado of convicted sail

Is scattered and disjoin'd from fellowship.

PANDULPH.

Courage and comfort! all shall yet go well.

KING PHILIP.

What can go well, when we have run so ill.

Are we not beaten? Is not Angiers lost?

Arthur ta'en prisoner? divers dear friends slain?

And bloody England into England gone,

O'erbearing interruption, spite of France?

LOUIS.

What he hath won, that hath he fortified:

So hot a speed with such advice dispos'd,

Such temperate order in so fierce a cause,

Doth want example: who hath read or heard

Of any kindred action like to this?

KING PHILIP.

Well could I bear that England had this praise,

So we could find some pattern of our shame.—

Look who comes here! a grave unto a soul;

Holding the eternal spirit, against her will,

In the vile prison of afflicted breath.

[Enter CONSTANCE.]

I pr'ythee, lady, go away with me.

CONSTANCE.

Lo, now! now see the issue of your peace!

KING PHILIP.

Patience, good lady! comfort, gentle Constance!

CONSTANCE.

No, I defy all counsel, all redress,

But that which ends all counsel, true redress,

Death, death:—O amiable lovely death!

Thou odoriferous stench! sound rottenness!

Arise forth from the couch of lasting night,

Thou hate and terror to prosperity,

And I will kiss thy detestable bones;

And put my eyeballs in thy vaulty brows;

And ring these fingers with thy household worms;

And stop this gap of breath with fulsome dust,

And be a carrion monster like thyself:

Come, grin on me; and I will think thou smil'st,

And buss thee as thy wife! Misery's love,

O, come to me!

KING PHILIP.

O fair affliction, peace!

CONSTANCE.

No, no, I will not, having breath to cry:—

O, that my tongue were in the thunder's mouth!

Then with a passion would I shake the world;

And rouse from sleep that fell anatomy

Which cannot hear a lady's feeble voice,

Which scorns a modern invocation.

PANDULPH.

Lady, you utter madness, and not sorrow.

CONSTANCE.

Thou art not holy to belie me so;

I am not mad: this hair I tear is mine;

My name is Constance; I was Geffrey's wife;

Young Arthur is my son, and he is lost:

I am not mad:—I would to heaven I were!

For then, 'tis like I should forget myself:

O, if I could, what grief should I forget!—

Preach some philosophy to make me mad,

And thou shalt be canoniz'd, cardinal;

For, being not mad, but sensible of grief,

My reasonable part produces reason

How I may be deliver'd of these woes,

And teaches me to kill or hang myself:

If I were mad I should forget my son,

Or madly think a babe of clouts were he:

I am not mad; too well, too well I feel

The different plague of each calamity.

KING PHILIP.

Bind up those tresses.—O, what love I note

In the fair multitude of those her hairs!

Where but by a chance a silver drop hath fallen,

Even to that drop ten thousand wiry friends

Do glue themselves in sociable grief;

Like true, inseparable, faithful loves,

Sticking together in calamity.

CONSTANCE.

To England, if you will.

KING PHILIP.

Bind up your hairs.

CONSTANCE.

Yes, that I will; and wherefore will I do it?

I tore them from their bonds, and cried aloud,

'O that these hands could so redeem my son,

87

As they have given these hairs their liberty!'

But now I envy at their liberty,

And will again commit them to their bonds,

Because my poor child is a prisoner.—

And, father cardinal, I have heard you say

That we shall see and know our friends in heaven:

If that be true, I shall see my boy again;

For since the birth of Cain, the first male child,

To him that did but yesterday suspire,

There was not such a gracious creature born.

But now will canker sorrow eat my bud,

And chase the native beauty from his cheek,

And he will look as hollow as a ghost,

As dim and meagre as an ague's fit;

And so he'll die; and, rising so again,

When I shall meet him in the court of heaven

I shall not know him: therefore never, never

Must I behold my pretty Arthur more!

PANDULPH.

You hold too heinous a respect of grief.

CONSTANCE.

He talks to me that never had a son.

KING PHILIP.

You are as fond of grief as of your child.

CONSTANCE.

Grief fills the room up of my absent child,

Lies in his bed, walks up and down with me,

Puts on his pretty looks, repeats his words,

Remembers me of all his gracious parts,

Stuffs out his vacant garments with his form;

Then have I reason to be fond of grief.

Fare you well: had you such a loss as I,

I could give better comfort than you do.—

I will not keep this form upon my head,

[Tearing off her head-dress.]

When there is such disorder in my wit.

O Lord! my boy, my Arthur, my fair son!

My life, my joy, my food, my ail the world!

My widow-comfort, and my sorrows' cure!

[Exit.]

KING PHILIP.

I fear some outrage, and I'll follow her.

[Exit.]

LOUIS.

There's nothing in this world can make me joy:

Life is as tedious as a twice-told tale

Vexing the dull ear of a drowsy man;

And bitter shame hath spoil'd the sweet world's taste,

That it yields nought but shame and bitterness.

PANDULPH.

Before the curing of a strong disease,

Even in the instant of repair and health,

The fit is strongest; evils that take leave

On their departure most of all show evil;

What have you lost by losing of this day?

LOUIS.

All days of glory, joy, and happiness.

PANDULPH.

If you had won it, certainly you had.

No, no; when Fortune means to men most good,

She looks upon them with a threatening eye.

'Tis strange to think how much King John hath lost

In this which he accounts so clearly won.

Are not you griev'd that Arthur is his prisoner?

LouIS.

As heartily as he is glad he hath him.

PANDULPH.

Your mind is all as youthful as your blood.

Now hear me speak with a prophetic spirit;

For even the breath of what I mean to speak

Shall blow each dust, each straw, each little rub,

Out of the path which shall directly lead

Thy foot to England's throne; and therefore mark.

John hath seiz'd Arthur; and it cannot be

That, whiles warm life plays in that infant's veins,

The misplac'd John should entertain an hour,

One minute, nay, one quiet breath of rest:

A sceptre snatch'd with an unruly hand

Must be boisterously maintain'd as gain'd:

And he that stands upon a slippery place

Makes nice of no vile hold to stay him up:

That John may stand then, Arthur needs must fall:

So be it, for it cannot be but so.

LOUIS.

But what shall I gain by young Arthur's fall?

PANDULPH.

You, in the right of Lady Blanch your wife,

May then make all the claim that Arthur did.

LOUIS.

And lose it, life and all, as Arthur did.

PANDULPH.

How green you are, and fresh in this old world!

John lays you plots; the times conspire with you;

For he that steeps his safety in true blood

Shall find but bloody safety and untrue.

This act, so evilly borne, shall cool the hearts

Of all his people, and freeze up their zeal,

That none so small advantage shall step forth

To check his reign, but they will cherish it;

No natural exhalation in the sky,

No scope of nature, no distemper'd day,

No common wind, no customed event,

But they will pluck away his natural cause

And call them meteors, prodigies, and signs,

Abortives, presages, and tongues of heaven,

Plainly denouncing vengeance upon John.

LOUIS.

May be he will not touch young Arthur's life,

But hold himself safe in his prisonment.

PANDULPH.

O, sir, when he shall hear of your approach,

If that young Arthur be not gone already,

Even at that news he dies; and then the hearts

Of all his people shall revolt from him,

And kiss the lips of unacquainted change;

And pick strong matter of revolt and wrath

Out of the bloody fingers' ends of john.

Methinks I see this hurly all on foot:

And, O, what better matter breeds for you

Than I have nam'd!—The bastard Falconbridge

Is now in England, ransacking the church,

Offending charity: if but a dozen French

Were there in arms, they would be as a call

To train ten thousand English to their side:

Or as a little snow, tumbled about

Anon becomes a mountain. O noble Dauphin,

Go with me to the king:—'tis wonderful

What may be wrought out of their discontent,

Now that their souls are topful of offence:

For England go:—I will whet on the king.

LOUIS.

Strong reasons makes strong actions: let us go:

If you say ay, the king will not say no.

[Exeunt.]

ACT IV.

SCENE 1. Northampton. A Room in the Castle.

[Enter HUBERT and two Attendants.]

HUBERT.

Heat me these irons hot; and look thou stand

Within the arras: when I strike my foot

Upon the bosom of the ground, rush forth

And bind the boy which you shall find with me

Fast to the chair: be heedful: hence, and watch.

FIRST ATTENDANT.

I hope your warrant will bear out the deed.

HUBERT.

Uncleanly scruples! Fear not you; look to't.—

[Exeunt ATTENDANTS.]

Young lad, come forth; I have to say with you.

[Enter ARTHUR.]

ARTHUR.

Good morrow, Hubert.

HUBERT.

Good morrow, little prince.

ARTHUR.

As little prince, having so great a tide

To be more prince, as may be.—You are sad.

HUBERT.

Indeed I have been merrier.

ARTHUR.

Mercy on me!

Methinks no body should be sad but I:

Yet, I remember, when I was in France,

Young gentlemen would be as sad as night,

Only for wantonness. By my christendom,

So I were out of prison, and kept sheep,

I should be as merry as the day is long;

And so I would be here, but that I doubt

My uncle practises more harm to me:

He is afraid of me, and I of him:

Is it my fault that I was Geffrey's son?

No, indeed, is't not; and I would to heaven

I were your son, so you would love me, Hubert.

HUBERT.

[Aside.] If I talk to him, with his innocent prate

He will awake my mercy, which lies dead:

Therefore I will be sudden and despatch.

ARTHUR.

Are you sick, Hubert? you look pale to-day:

In sooth, I would you were a little sick,

That I might sit all night and watch with you:

I warrant I love you more than you do me.

HUBERT.

[Aside.] His words do take possession of my bosom.—

Read here, young Arthur.

[Showing a paper.]

[Aside.] How now, foolish rheum!

Turning dispiteous torture out of door!

I must be brief, lest resolution drop

Out at mine eyes in tender womanish tears.—

Can you not read it? is it not fair writ?

ARTHUR.

Too fairly, Hubert, for so foul effect.

Must you with hot irons burn out both mine eyes?

HUBERT.

Young boy, I must.

ARTHUR.

And will you?

HUBERT.

And I will.

ARTHUR.

Have you the heart? When your head did but ache,

I knit my handkerchief about your brows,—

The best I had, a princess wrought it me,—

And I did never ask it you again;

And with my hand at midnight held your head;

And, like the watchful minutes to the hour,

Still and anon cheer'd up the heavy time,

Saying 'What lack you?' and 'Where lies your grief?'

Or 'What good love may I perform for you?'

Many a poor man's son would have lien still,

And ne'er have spoke a loving word to you;

But you at your sick service had a prince.

Nay, you may think my love was crafty love,

And call it cunning.—do, an if you will:

If heaven be pleas'd that you must use me ill,

Why, then you must.—Will you put out mine eyes,

These eyes that never did nor never shall

So much as frown on you?

HUBERT.

I have sworn to do it!

And with hot irons must I burn them out.

ARTHUR.

Ah, none but in this iron age would do it!

The iron of itself, though heat red-hot,

Approaching near these eyes would drink my tears,

And quench his fiery indignation,

Even in the matter of mine innocence;

Nay, after that, consume away in rust,

But for containing fire to harm mine eye.

Are you more stubborn-hard than hammer'd iron?

An if an angel should have come to me

And told me Hubert should put out mine eyes,

I would not have believ'd him,—no tongue but Hubert's.

HUBERT.

[Stamps.] Come forth.

[Re-enter Attendants, with cords, irons, &c.]

Do as I bid you do.

ARTHUR.

O, save me, Hubert, save me! my eyes are out

Even with the fierce looks of these bloody men.

HUBERT.

Give me the iron, I say, and bind him here.

ARTHUR.

Alas, what need you be so boist'rous rough?

I will not struggle, I will stand stone-still.

For heaven sake, Hubert, let me not be bound!

Nay, hear me, Hubert!—drive these men away,

And I will sit as quiet as a lamb;

I will not stir, nor wince, nor speak a word,

Nor look upon the iron angerly:

Thrust but these men away, and I'll forgive you,

Whatever torment you do put me to.

HUBERT.

Go, stand within; let me alone with him.

FIRST ATTENDANT.

I am best pleas'd to be from such a deed.

[Exeunt Attendants.]

ARTHUR.

Alas, I then have chid away my friend!

He hath a stern look but a gentle heart:—

Let him come back, that his compassion may

Give life to yours.

HUBERT.

Come, boy, prepare yourself.

ARTHUR.

Is there no remedy?

HUBERT.

None, but to lose your eyes.

ARTHUR.

O heaven!—that there were but a mote in yours,

A grain, a dust, a gnat, a wandering hair,

Any annoyance in that precious sense!

Then, feeling what small things are boisterous there,

Your vile intent must needs seem horrible.

HUBERT.

Is this your promise? go to, hold your tongue.

ARTHUR.

Hubert, the utterance of a brace of tongues

Must needs want pleading for a pair of eyes:

Let me not hold my tongue,—let me not, Hubert;

Or, Hubert, if you will, cut out my tongue,

So I may keep mine eyes: O, spare mine eyes,

Though to no use but still to look on you!—

Lo, by my troth, the instrument is cold

And would not harm me.

HUBERT.

I can heat it, boy.

ARTHUR.

No, in good sooth; the fire is dead with grief,

Being create for comfort, to be us'd

In undeserv'd extremes: see else yourself;

There is no malice in this burning coal;

The breath of heaven hath blown his spirit out,

And strew'd repentant ashes on his head.

HUBERT.

But with my breath I can revive it, boy.

ARTHUR.

An if you do, you will but make it blush,

And glow with shame of your proceedings, Hubert.

Nay, it, perchance will sparkle in your eyes;

And, like a dog that is compell'd to fight,

Snatch at his master that doth tarre him on.

All things that you should use to do me wrong,

Deny their office: only you do lack

That mercy which fierce fire and iron extends,

Creatures of note for mercy-lacking uses.

HUBERT.

Well, see to live; I will not touch thine eye

For all the treasure that thine uncle owes:

Yet I am sworn, and I did purpose, boy,

With this same very iron to burn them out.

ARTHUR.

O, now you look like Hubert! all this while

You were disguised.

HUBERT.

Peace; no more. Adieu!

Your uncle must not know but you are dead;

I'll fill these dogged spies with false reports:

And, pretty child, sleep doubtless and secure

That Hubert, for the wealth of all the world,

Will not offend thee.

ARTHUR.

O heaven! I thank you, Hubert.

HUBERT.

Silence; no more: go closely in with me:

Much danger do I undergo for thee.

[Exeunt.]

SCENE 2.The same. A Room of State in the Palace.

[Enter KING JOHN, crowned, PEMBROKE, SALISBURY, and other LORDS. The KING takes his State.]

KING JOHN.

Here once again we sit, once again crown'd,

And look'd upon, I hope, with cheerful eyes.

PEMBROKE.

This once again, but that your highness pleas'd,

Was once superfluous: you were crown'd before,

And that high royalty was ne'er pluck'd off;

The faiths of men ne'er stained with revolt;

Fresh expectation troubled not the land

With any long'd-for change or better state.

SALISBURY.

Therefore, to be possess'd with double pomp,

To guard a title that was rich before,

To gild refined gold, to paint the lily,

To throw a perfume on the violet,

To smooth the ice, or add another hue

Unto the rainbow, or with taper-light

To seek the beauteous eye of heaven to garnish,

Is wasteful and ridiculous excess.

PEMBROKE.

But that your royal pleasure must be done,

This act is as an ancient tale new told;

And, in the last repeating troublesome,

Being urged at a time unseasonable.

SALISBURY.

In this, the antique and well-noted face

Of plain old form is much disfigured;

And, like a shifted wind unto a sail,

It makes the course of thoughts to fetch about;

Startles and frights consideration;

Makes sound opinion sick, and truth suspected,

For putting on so new a fashion'd robe.

PEMBROKE.

When workmen strive to do better than well,

They do confound their skill in covetousness;

And oftentimes excusing of a fault

Doth make the fault the worse by the excuse,—

As patches set upon a little breach

Discredit more in hiding of the fault

Than did the fault before it was so patch'd.

SALISBURY.

To this effect, before you were new-crown'd,

We breath'd our counsel: but it pleas'd your highness

To overbear it; and we are all well pleas'd,

Since all and every part of what we would

Doth make a stand at what your highness will.

KING JOHN.

Some reasons of this double coronation

I have possess'd you with, and think them strong;

And more, more strong, when lesser is my fear,

I shall indue you with: meantime but ask

What you would have reform'd that is not well,

And well shall you perceive how willingly

I will both hear and grant you your requests.

PEMBROKE.

Then I,—as one that am the tongue of these,

To sound the purposes of all their hearts,—

Both for myself and them,—but, chief of all,

Your safety, for the which myself and them

Bend their best studies,—heartily request

The enfranchisement of Arthur, whose restraint

Doth move the murmuring lips of discontent

To break into this dangerous argument,—

If what in rest you have in right you hold,

Why then your fears,—which, as they say, attend

The steps of wrong,—should move you to mew up

Your tender kinsman, and to choke his days

With barbarous ignorance, and deny his youth

The rich advantage of good exercise?

That the time's enemies may not have this

To grace occasions, let it be our suit

That you have bid us ask his liberty;

Which for our goods we do no further ask

Than whereupon our weal, on you depending,

Counts it your weal he have his liberty.

KING JOHN.

Let it be so: I do commit his youth

To your direction.

[Enter HUBERT.]

Hubert, what news with you?

PEMBROKE.

This is the man should do the bloody deed;

He show'd his warrant to a friend of mine:

The image of a wicked heinous fault

Lives in his eye; that close aspect of his

Doth show the mood of a much-troubled breast;

And I do fearfully believe 'tis done

What we so fear'd he had a charge to do.

SALISBURY.

The colour of the king doth come and go

Between his purpose and his conscience,

Like heralds 'twixt two dreadful battles set.

His passion is so ripe it needs must break.

PEMBROKE.

And when it breaks, I fear will issue thence

The foul corruption of a sweet child's death.

KING JOHN.

We cannot hold mortality's strong hand:—

Good lords, although my will to give is living,

The suit which you demand is gone and dead:

He tells us Arthur is deceas'd to-night.

SALISBURY.

Indeed, we fear'd his sickness was past cure.

PEMBROKE.

Indeed, we heard how near his death he was,

Before the child himself felt he was sick:

This must be answer'd either here or hence.

KING JOHN.

Why do you bend such solemn brows on me?

Think you I bear the shears of destiny?

Have I commandment on the pulse of life?

SALISBURY.

It is apparent foul-play; and 'tis shame

That greatness should so grossly offer it:

So thrive it in your game! and so, farewell.

PEMBROKE.

Stay yet, Lord Salisbury, I'll go with thee

And find th' inheritance of this poor child,

His little kingdom of a forced grave.

That blood which ow'd the breadth of all this isle

Three foot of it doth hold:—bad world the while!

This must not be thus borne: this will break out

To all our sorrows, and ere long, I doubt.

[Exeunt LORDS.]

KING JOHN.

They burn in indignation. I repent:

There is no sure foundation set on blood;

No certain life achiev'd by others' death.—

[Enter a MESSENGER.]

A fearful eye thou hast: where is that blood

That I have seen inhabit in those cheeks?

So foul a sky clears not without a storm:

Pour down thy weather:—how goes all in France?

MESSENGER.

From France to England.—Never such a power

For any foreign preparation

Was levied in the body of a land.

The copy of your speed is learn'd by them;

For when you should be told they do prepare,

The tidings comes that they are all arriv'd.

KING JOHN.

O, where hath our intelligence been drunk?

Where hath it slept? Where is my mother's care,

That such an army could be drawn in France,

And she not hear of it?

MESSENGER.

My liege, her ear

Is stopp'd with dust; the first of April died

Your noble mother; and as I hear, my lord,

The Lady Constance in a frenzy died

Three days before; but this from rumour's tongue

I idly heard,—if true or false I know not.

KING JOHN.

Withhold thy speed, dreadful occasion!

O, make a league with me, till I have pleas'd

My discontented peers!—What! mother dead!

How wildly, then, walks my estate in France!—

Under whose conduct came those powers of France

That thou for truth giv'st out are landed here?

MESSENGER.

Under the Dauphin.

KING JOHN.

Thou hast made me giddy

With these in tidings.

[Enter the BASTARD and PETER OF POMFRET.]

Now! What says the world

To your proceedings? do not seek to stuff

My head with more ill news, for it is full.

BASTARD.

But if you be afear'd to hear the worst,

Then let the worst, unheard, fall on your head.

KING JOHN.

Bear with me, cousin, for I was amaz'd

Under the tide: but now I breathe again

Aloft the flood; and can give audience

To any tongue, speak it of what it will.

BASTARD.

How I have sped among the clergymen,

The sums I have collected shall express.

But as I travell'd hither through the land,

I find the people strangely fantasied;

Possess'd with rumours, full of idle dreams.

Not knowing what they fear, but full of fear;

110

And here's a prophet that I brought with me

From forth the streets of Pomfret, whom I found

With many hundreds treading on his heels;

To whom he sung, in rude harsh-sounding rhymes,

That, ere the next Ascension-day at noon,

Your highness should deliver up your crown.

KING JOHN.

Thou idle dreamer, wherefore didst thou so?

PETER.

Foreknowing that the truth will fall out so.

KING JOHN.

Hubert, away with him; imprison him;

And on that day at noon, whereon he says

I shall yield up my crown, let him be hang'd.

Deliver him to safety; and return,

For I must use thee.

[Exit HUBERT with PETER.]

O my gentle cousin,

Hear'st thou the news abroad, who are arriv'd?

BASTARD.

The French, my lord; men's mouths are full of it;

Besides, I met Lord Bigot and Lord Salisbury,—

With eyes as red as new-enkindled fire,

And others more, going to seek the grave

Of Arthur, whom they say is kill'd to-night

On your suggestion.

KING JOHN.

Gentle kinsman, go

And thrust thyself into their companies:

I have a way to will their loves again:

Bring them before me.

BASTARD.

I will seek them out.

KING JOHN.

Nay, but make haste; the better foot before.

O, let me have no subject enemies

When adverse foreigners affright my towns

With dreadful pomp of stout invasion!

Be Mercury, set feathers to thy heels,

And fly like thought from them to me again.

BASTARD.

The spirit of the time shall teach me speed.

KING JOHN.

Spoke like a sprightful noble gentleman!

[Exit BASTARD.]

Go after him; for he perhaps shall need

Some messenger betwixt me and the peers;

And be thou he.

MESSENGER.

With all my heart, my liege.

[Exit.]

KING JOHN.

My mother dead!

[Re-enter HUBERT.]

HUBERT.

My lord, they say five moons were seen to-night;

Four fixed, and the fifth did whirl about

The other four in wondrous motion.

KING JOHN.

Five moons!

HUBERT.

Old men and beldams in the streets

Do prophesy upon it dangerously:

Young Arthur's death is common in their mouths:

And when they talk of him, they shake their heads,

And whisper one another in the ear;

And he that speaks doth gripe the hearer's wrist;

Whilst he that hears makes fearful action

With wrinkled brows, with nods, with rolling eyes.

I saw a smith stand with his hammer, thus,

The whilst his iron did on the anvil cool,

With open mouth swallowing a tailor's news;

113

Who, with his shears and measure in his hand,

Standing on slippers,—which his nimble haste

Had falsely thrust upon contrary feet,—

Told of a many thousand warlike French

That were embattailed and rank'd in Kent.

Another lean unwash'd artificer

Cuts off his tale, and talks of Arthur's death.

KING JOHN.

Why seek'st thou to possess me with these fears?

Why urgest thou so oft young Arthur's death?

Thy hand hath murder'd him: I had a mighty cause

To wish him dead, but thou hadst none to kill him.

HUBERT.

No had, my lord! why, did you not provoke me?

KING JOHN.

It is the curse of kings to be attended

By slaves that take their humours for a warrant

To break within the bloody house of life;

And, on the winking of authority,

To understand a law; to know the meaning

Of dangerous majesty, when perchance it frowns

More upon humour than advis'd respect.

HUBERT.

Here is your hand and seal for what I did.

KING JOHN.

O, when the last account 'twixt heaven and earth

Is to be made, then shall this hand and seal

Witness against us to damnation!

How oft the sight of means to do ill deeds

Make deeds ill done! Hadst not thou been by,

A fellow by the hand of nature mark'd,

Quoted and sign'd to do a deed of shame,

This murder had not come into my mind:

But, taking note of thy abhorr'd aspect,

Finding thee fit for bloody villainy,

Apt, liable to be employ'd in danger,

I faintly broke with thee of Arthur's death;

And thou, to be endeared to a king,

Made it no conscience to destroy a prince.

HUBERT.

My lord,—

KING JOHN.

Hadst thou but shook thy head or made pause,

When I spake darkly what I purpos'd,

Or turn'd an eye of doubt upon my face,

As bid me tell my tale in express words,

Deep shame had struck me dumb, made me break off,

And those thy fears might have wrought fears in me:

But thou didst understand me by my signs,

And didst in signs again parley with sin;

Yea, without stop, didst let thy heart consent,

And consequently thy rude hand to act

The deed which both our tongues held vile to name.—

Out of my sight, and never see me more!

My nobles leave me; and my state is brav'd,

Even at my gates, with ranks of foreign powers;

Nay, in the body of the fleshly land,

This kingdom, this confine of blood and breath,

Hostility and civil tumult reigns

Between my conscience and my cousin's death.

HUBERT.

Arm you against your other enemies,

I'll make a peace between your soul and you.

Young Arthur is alive: this hand of mine

Is yet a maiden and an innocent hand,

Not painted with the crimson spots of blood.

Within this bosom never enter'd yet

The dreadful motion of a murderous thought;

And you have slander'd nature in my form,—

Which, howsoever rude exteriorly,

Is yet the cover of a fairer mind

Than to be butcher of an innocent child.

KING JOHN.

Doth Arthur live? O, haste thee to the peers,

Throw this report on their incensed rage,

And make them tame to their obedience!

Forgive the comment that my passion made

Upon thy feature; for my rage was blind,

And foul imaginary eyes of blood

Presented thee more hideous than thou art.

O, answer not; but to my closet bring

The angry lords with all expedient haste:

I conjure thee but slowly; run more fast.

[Exeunt.]

SCENE 3. The same. Before the castle.

[Enter ARTHUR, on the Walls.]

ARTHUR.

The wall is high, and yet will I leap down:—

Good ground, be pitiful and hurt me not!—

There's few or none do know me: if they did,

This ship-boy's semblance hath disguis'd me quite.

I am afraid; and yet I'll venture it.

If I get down, and do not break my limbs,

I'll find a thousand shifts to get away:

As good to die and go, as die and stay.

[Leaps down.]

O me! my uncle's spirit is in these stones:—

Heaven take my soul, and England keep my bones!

[Dies.]

[Enter PEMBROKE, SALISBURY, and BIGOT.]

SALISBURY.

Lords, I will meet him at Saint Edmunds-Bury;

It is our safety, and we must embrace

This gentle offer of the perilous time.

PEMBROKE.

Who brought that letter from the cardinal?

SALISBURY.

The Count Melun, a noble lord of France,

Whose private with me of the Dauphin's love

Is much more general than these lines import.

BIGOT.

To-morrow morning let us meet him then.

SALISBURY.

Or rather then set forward; for 'twill be

Two long days' journey, lords, or e'er we meet.

[Enter the BASTARD.]

BASTARD.

Once more to-day well met, distemper'd lords!

The king by me requests your presence straight.

SALISBURY.

The King hath dispossess'd himself of us.

We will not line his thin bestained cloak

With our pure honours, nor attend the foot

That leaves the print of blood where'er it walks.

Return and tell him so: we know the worst.

BASTARD.

Whate'er you think, good words, I think, were best.

SALISBURY.

Our griefs, and not our manners, reason now.

BASTARD.

But there is little reason in your grief;

Therefore 'twere reason you had manners now.

PEMBROKE.

Sir, sir, impatience hath his privilege.

BASTARD.

'Tis true,—to hurt his master, no man else.

SALISBURY.

This is the prison:—what is he lies here?

[Seeing Arthur.]

PEMBROKE.

O death, made proud with pure and princely beauty!

The earth had not a hole to hide this deed.

SALISBURY.

Murder, as hating what himself hath done,

Doth lay it open to urge on revenge.

BIGOT.

Or, when he doom'd this beauty to a grave,

Found it too precious-princely for a grave.

SALISBURY.

Sir Richard, what think you? Have you beheld,

Or have you read or heard, or could you think?

Or do you almost think, although you see,

That you do see? could thought, without this object,

Form such another? This is the very top,

The height, the crest, or crest unto the crest,

Of murder's arms: this is the bloodiest shame,

The wildest savagery, the vilest stroke,

That ever wall-ey'd wrath or staring rage

Presented to the tears of soft remorse.

PEMBROKE.

All murders past do stand excus'd in this;

And this, so sole and so unmatchable,

Shall give a holiness, a purity,

To the yet unbegotten sin of times;

And prove a deadly bloodshed but a jest,

Exampled by this heinous spectacle.

BASTARD.

It is a damned and a bloody work;

The graceless action of a heavy hand,—

If that it be the work of any hand.

SALISBURY.

If that it be the work of any hand?—

We had a kind of light what would ensue.

It is the shameful work of Hubert's hand;

The practice and the purpose of the king:—

From whose obedience I forbid my soul,

Kneeling before this ruin of sweet life,

And breathing to his breathless excellence

The incense of a vow, a holy vow,

Never to taste the pleasures of the world,

Never to be infected with delight,

Nor conversant with ease and idleness,

Till I have set a glory to this hand,

By giving it the worship of revenge.

PEMBROKE. and BIGOT.

Our souls religiously confirm thy words.

[Enter HUBERT.]

HUBERT.

Lords, I am hot with haste in seeking you:

Arthur doth live; the king hath sent for you.

SALISBURY.

O, he is bold, and blushes not at death:—

Avaunt, thou hateful villain, get thee gone!

HUBERT.

I am no villain.

SALISBURY.

Must I rob the law?

[Drawing his sword.]

BASTARD.

Your sword is bright, sir; put it up again.

SALISBURY.

Not till I sheathe it in a murderer's skin.

HUBERT.

Stand back, Lord Salisbury,—stand back, I say;

By heaven, I think my sword's as sharp as yours:

I would not have you, lord, forget yourself,

Nor tempt the danger of my true defence;

Lest I, by marking of your rage, forget

Your worth, your greatness, and nobility.

BIGOT.

Out, dunghill! dar'st thou brave a nobleman?

HUBERT.

Not for my life: but yet I dare defend

My innocent life against an emperor.

SALISBURY.

Thou art a murderer.

HUBERT.

Do not prove me so;

Yet I am none: whose tongue soe'er speaks false,

Not truly speaks; who speaks not truly, lies.

PEMBROKE.

Cut him to pieces.

BASTARD.

Keep the peace, I say.

SALISBURY.

Stand by, or I shall gall you, Falconbridge.

BASTARD.

Thou wert better gall the devil, Salisbury:

If thou but frown on me, or stir thy foot,

Or teach thy hasty spleen to do me shame,

I'll strike thee dead. Put up thy sword betime:

Or I'll so maul you and your toasting-iron

That you shall think the devil is come from hell.

BIGOT.

What wilt thou do, renowned Falconbridge?

Second a villain and a murderer?

HUBERT.

Lord Bigot, I am none.

BIGOT.

Who kill'd this prince?

HUBERT.

'Tis not an hour since I left him well:

I honour'd him, I lov'd him, and will weep

My date of life out for his sweet life's loss.

SALISBURY.

Trust not those cunning waters of his eyes,

For villainy is not without such rheum;

And he, long traded in it, makes it seem

Like rivers of remorse and innocency.

Away with me, all you whose souls abhor

Th' uncleanly savours of a slaughter-house;

For I am stifled with this smell of sin.

BIGOT.

Away toward Bury, to the Dauphin there!

PEMBROKE.

There tell the king he may inquire us out.

[Exeunt LORDS.]

BASTARD.

Here's a good world!—Knew you of this fair work?

Beyond the infinite and boundless reach

Of mercy, if thou didst this deed of death,

Art thou damn'd, Hubert.

HUBERT.

Do but hear me, sir.

BASTARD.

Ha! I'll tell thee what;

Thou'rt damn'd as black—nay, nothing is so black;

Thou art more deep damn'd than Prince Lucifer:

There is not yet so ugly a fiend of hell

As thou shalt be, if thou didst kill this child.

HUBERT.

Upon my soul,—

BASTARD.

If thou didst but consent

To this most cruel act, do but despair;

And if thou want'st a cord, the smallest thread

That ever spider twisted from her womb

Will serve to strangle thee; a rush will be a beam

To hang thee on; or wouldst thou drown thyself,

Put but a little water in a spoon

And it shall be as all the ocean,

Enough to stifle such a villain up.

I do suspect thee very grievously.

HUBERT.

If I in act, consent, or sin of thought,

Be guilty of the stealing that sweet breath

Which was embounded in this beauteous clay,

Let hell want pains enough to torture me!

I left him well.

BASTARD.

Go, bear him in thine arms.—

I am amaz'd, methinks, and lose my way

Among the thorns and dangers of this world.—

How easy dost thou take all England up!

From forth this morsel of dead royalty,

The life, the right, and truth of all this realm

Is fled to heaven; and England now is left

To tug and scamble, and to part by the teeth

The unow'd interest of proud-swelling state.

Now for the bare-pick'd bone of majesty

Doth dogged war bristle his angry crest,

And snarleth in the gentle eyes of peace:

Now powers from home and discontents at home

Meet in one line; and vast confusion waits,

As doth a raven on a sick-fallen beast,

The imminent decay of wrested pomp.

Now happy he whose cloak and cincture can

Hold out this tempest.—Bear away that child,

And follow me with speed: I'll to the king;

A thousand businesses are brief in hand,

And heaven itself doth frown upon the land.

[Exeunt.]

ACT V.

SCENE 1. Northampton. A Room in the Palace.

[Enter **KING JOHN, PANDULPH** with the crown, and Attendants.]

KING JOHN.

Thus have I yielded up into your hand

The circle of my glory.

PANDULPH.

[Give KING JOHN the crown.]

Take again

From this my hand, as holding of the pope,

Your sovereign greatness and authority.

KING JOHN.

Now keep your holy word: go meet the French;

And from his holiness use all your power

To stop their marches 'fore we are inflam'd.

Our discontented counties do revolt;

Our people quarrel with obedience;

Swearing allegiance and the love of soul

To stranger blood, to foreign royalty.

This inundation of mistemper'd humour

Rests by you only to be qualified.

Then pause not; for the present time's so sick

That present medicine must be ministr'd

Or overthrow incurable ensues.

PANDULPH.

It was my breath that blew this tempest up,

Upon your stubborn usage of the pope:

But since you are a gentle convertite,

My tongue shall hush again this storm of war

And make fair weather in your blustering land.

On this Ascension-day, remember well,

Upon your oath of service to the pope,

Go I to make the French lay down their arms.

[Exit.]

KING JOHN.

Is this Ascension-day? Did not the prophet

Say that before Ascension-day at noon

My crown I should give off? Even so I have:

I did suppose it should be on constraint;

But, heaven be thank'd, it is but voluntary.

[Enter the BASTARD.]

BASTARD.

All Kent hath yielded; nothing there holds out

But Dover Castle: London hath receiv'd,

Like a kind host, the Dauphin and his powers:

Your nobles will not hear you, but are gone

To offer service to your enemy;

And wild amazement hurries up and down

The little number of your doubtful friends.

KING JOHN.

Would not my lords return to me again

After they heard young Arthur was alive?

BASTARD.

They found him dead, and cast into the streets;

An empty casket, where the jewel of life

By some damn'd hand was robb'd and ta'en away.

KING JOHN.

That villain Hubert told me he did live.

BASTARD.

So, on my soul, he did, for aught he knew.

But wherefore do you droop? why look you sad?

Be great in act, as you have been in thought;

Let not the world see fear and sad distrust

Govern the motion of a kingly eye:

Be stirring as the time; be fire with fire;

Threaten the threatener, and outface the brow

Of bragging horror: so shall inferior eyes,

That borrow their behaviours from the great,

Grow great by your example, and put on

The dauntless spirit of resolution.

Away, and glister like the god of war

When he intendeth to become the field:

Show boldness and aspiring confidence.

What, shall they seek the lion in his den,

And fright him there? and make him tremble there?

O, let it not be said!—Forage, and run

To meet displeasure farther from the doors,

And grapple with him ere he come so nigh.

KING JOHN.

The legate of the pope hath been with me,

And I have made a happy peace with him;

And he hath promis'd to dismiss the powers

Led by the Dauphin.

BASTARD.

O inglorious league!

Shall we, upon the footing of our land,

Send fair-play orders, and make compromise,

Insinuation, parley, and base truce,

To arms invasive? shall a beardless boy,

A cocker'd silken wanton, brave our fields,

And flesh his spirit in a warlike soil,

Mocking the air with colours idly spread,

And find no check? Let us, my liege, to arms;

Perchance the cardinal cannot make your peace;

Or, if he do, let it at least be said

They saw we had a purpose of defence.

KING JOHN.

Have thou the ordering of this present time.

BASTARD.

Away, then, with good courage! yet, I know

Our party may well meet a prouder foe.

[Exeunt.]

SCENE 2. Near Saint Edmunds-bury. The French Camp.

[Enter, in arms, LOUIS, SALISBURY, MELUN, PEMBROKE, BIGOT, and soldiers.]

LOUIS.

My Lord Melun, let this be copied out

And keep it safe for our remembrance:

Return the precedent to these lords again;

That, having our fair order written down,

Both they and we, perusing o'er these notes,

May know wherefore we took the sacrament,

And keep our faiths firm and inviolable.

SALISBURY.

Upon our sides it never shall be broken.

And, noble Dauphin, albeit we swear

A voluntary zeal and an unurg'd faith

To your proceedings; yet, believe me, prince,

I am not glad that such a sore of time

Should seek a plaster by contemn'd revolt,

And heal the inveterate canker of one wound

By making many. O, it grieves my soul

That I must draw this metal from my side

To be a widow-maker! O, and there

Where honourable rescue and defence

Cries out upon the name of Salisbury!

But such is the infection of the time,

That, for the health and physic of our right,

We cannot deal but with the very hand

Of stern injustice and confused wrong.—

And is't not pity, O my grieved friends!

That we, the sons and children of this isle,

Were born to see so sad an hour as this;

Wherein we step after a stranger-march

Upon her gentle bosom, and fill up

Her enemies' ranks—I must withdraw and weep

Upon the spot of this enforc'd cause—

To grace the gentry of a land remote,

And follow unacquainted colours here?

What, here?—O nation, that thou couldst remove!

That Neptune's arms, who clippeth thee about,

Would bear thee from the knowledge of thyself,

And grapple thee unto a pagan shore,

Where these two Christian armies might combine

The blood of malice in a vein of league,

And not to spend it so unneighbourly!

LOUIS.

A noble temper dost thou show in this;

And great affections wrestling in thy bosom

Doth make an earthquake of nobility.

O, what a noble combat hast thou fought

Between compulsion and a brave respect!

Let me wipe off this honourable dew

That silverly doth progress on thy cheeks:

My heart hath melted at a lady's tears,

Being an ordinary inundation;

But this effusion of such manly drops,

This shower, blown up by tempest of the soul,

Startles mine eyes and makes me more amaz'd

Than had I seen the vaulty top of heaven

Figur'd quite o'er with burning meteors.

Lift up thy brow, renowned Salisbury,

And with a great heart heave away this storm:

Commend these waters to those baby eyes

That never saw the giant world enrag'd,

Nor met with fortune other than at feasts,

Full of warm blood, of mirth, of gossiping.

Come, come; for thou shalt thrust thy hand as deep

Into the purse of rich prosperity

As Louis himself:—so, nobles, shall you all,

That knit your sinews to the strength of mine.—

And even there, methinks, an angel spake:

Look, where the holy legate comes apace,

To give us warrant from the hand of heaven

And on our actions set the name of right

With holy breath.

[Enter PANDULPH, attended.]

PANDULPH.

Hail, noble prince of France!

The next is this,—King John hath reconcil'd

Himself to Rome; his spirit is come in,

That so stood out against the holy church,

The great metropolis and see of Rome:

Therefore thy threatening colours now wind up,

And tame the savage spirit of wild war,

That, like a lion foster'd up at hand,

It may lie gently at the foot of peace

And be no further harmful than in show.

LOUIS.

Your grace shall pardon me, I will not back:

I am too high-born to be propertied,

To be a secondary at control,

Or useful serving-man and instrument

To any sovereign state throughout the world.

Your breath first kindled the dead coal of wars

Between this chastis'd kingdom and myself,

And brought in matter that should feed this fire;

And now 'tis far too huge to be blown out

With that same weak wind which enkindled it.

You taught me how to know the face of right,

Acquainted me with interest to this land,

Yea, thrust this enterprise into my heart;

And come ye now to tell me John hath made

His peace with Rome? What is that peace to me?

I, by the honour of my marriage-bed,

After young Arthur, claim this land for mine;

And, now it is half-conquer'd, must I back

Because that John hath made his peace with Rome?

Am I Rome's slave? What penny hath Rome borne,

What men provided, what munition sent,

To underprop this action? Is't not I

That undergo this charge? Who else but I,

And such as to my claim are liable,

Sweat in this business and maintain this war?

Have I not heard these islanders shout out,

'Vive le roi!' as I have bank'd their towns?

Have I not here the best cards for the game,

137

To will this easy match, play'd for a crown?

And shall I now give o'er the yielded set?

No, no, on my soul, it never shall be said.

PANDULPH.

You look but on the outside of this work.

LOUIS.

Outside or inside, I will not return

Till my attempt so much be glorified

As to my ample hope was promised

Before I drew this gallant head of war,

And cull'd these fiery spirits from the world,

To outlook conquest, and to will renown

Even in the jaws of danger and of death.—

[Trumpet sounds.]

What lusty trumpet thus doth summon us?

[Enter the BASTARD, attended.]

BASTARD.

According to the fair play of the world,

Let me have audience; I am sent to speak:—

My holy lord of Milan, from the king

I come, to learn how you have dealt for him;

And, as you answer, I do know the scope

And warrant limited unto my tongue.

PANDULPH.

The Dauphin is too wilful-opposite,

And will not temporize with my entreaties;

He flatly says he'll not lay down his arms.

BASTARD.

By all the blood that ever fury breath'd,

The youth says well.—Now hear our English king;

For thus his royalty doth speak in me.

He is prepar'd; and reason too he should:

This apish and unmannerly approach,

This harness'd masque and unadvised revel

This unhair'd sauciness and boyish troops,

The king doth smile at; and is well prepar'd

To whip this dwarfish war, these pigmy arms,

From out the circle of his territories.

That hand which had the strength, even at your door,

To cudgel you, and make you take the hatch;

To dive, like buckets, in concealed wells;

To crouch in litter of your stable planks;

To lie, like pawns, lock'd up in chests and trunks;

To hug with swine; to seek sweet safety out

In vaults and prisons; and to thrill and shake

Even at the crying of your nation's crow,

Thinking this voice an armed Englishman;—

Shall that victorious hand be feebled here

That in your chambers gave you chastisement?

No: know the gallant monarch is in arms

And like an eagle o'er his aery towers

To souse annoyance that comes near his nest.—

And you degenerate, you ingrate revolts,

You bloody Neroes, ripping up the womb

Of your dear mother England, blush for shame;

For your own ladies and pale-visag'd maids,

Like Amazons, come tripping after drums,—

Their thimbles into armed gauntlets chang'd,

Their needles to lances, and their gentle hearts

To fierce and bloody inclination.

LOUIS.

There end thy brave, and turn thy face in peace;

We grant thou canst outscold us: fare thee well;

We hold our time too precious to be spent

With such a brabbler.

PANDULPH.

Give me leave to speak.

BASTARD.

No, I will speak.

LOUIS.

We will attend to neither.—

Strike up the drums; and let the tongue of war,

Plead for our interest and our being here.

BASTARD.

Indeed, your drums, being beaten, will cry out;

And so shall you, being beaten: do but start

And echo with the clamour of thy drum,

And even at hand a drum is ready brac'd

That shall reverberate all as loud as thine:

Sound but another, and another shall,

As loud as thine, rattle the welkin's ear,

And mock the deep-mouth'd thunder: for at hand,—

Not trusting to this halting legate here,

Whom he hath us'd rather for sport than need,—

Is warlike John; and in his forehead sits

A bare-ribb'd death, whose office is this day

To feast upon whole thousands of the French.

LOUIS.

Strike up our drums, to find this danger out.

BASTARD.

And thou shalt find it, Dauphin, do not doubt.

[Exeunt.]

SCENE 3. The same. The Field of Battle.

[Alarums. Enter KING JOHN and HUBERT.]

KING JOHN.

How goes the day with us? O, tell me, Hubert.

HUBERT.

Badly, I fear. How fares your majesty?

KING JOHN.

This fever that hath troubled me so long

Lies heavy on me;—O, my heart is sick!

[Enter a MESSENGER.]

MESSENGER.

My lord, your valiant kinsman, Falconbridge,

Desires your majesty to leave the field

And send him word by me which way you go.

KING JOHN.

Tell him, toward Swinstead, to the abbey there.

MESSENGER.

Be of good comfort; for the great supply

That was expected by the Dauphin here

Are wreck'd three nights ago on Goodwin Sands.

This news was brought to Richard but even now:

The French fight coldly, and retire themselves.

KING JOHN.

Ay me! this tyrant fever burns me up

And will not let me welcome this good news.—

Set on toward Swinstead: to my litter straight;

Weakness possesseth me, and I am faint.

[Exeunt.]

SCENE 4. The same. Another part of the same.

[Enter SALISBURY, PEMBROKE, and others.]

SALISBURY.

I did not think the king so stor'd with friends.

PEMBROKE.

Up once again; put spirit in the French;

If they miscarry, we miscarry too.

SALISBURY.

That misbegotten devil, Falconbridge,

In spite of spite, alone upholds the day.

PEMBROKE.

They say King John, sore sick, hath left the field.

[Enter MELUN wounded, and led by Soldiers.]

MELUN.

Lead me to the revolts of England here.

SALISBURY.

When we were happy we had other names.

PEMBROKE.

It is the Count Melun.

SALISBURY.

Wounded to death.

MELUN.

Fly, noble English, you are bought and sold;

Unthread the rude eye of rebellion,

And welcome home again discarded faith.

Seek out King John, and fall before his feet;

For if the French be lords of this loud day,

He means to recompense the pains you take

By cutting off your heads: thus hath he sworn,

And I with him, and many more with me,

Upon the altar at Saint Edmunds-bury;

Even on that altar where we swore to you

Dear amity and everlasting love.

SALISBURY.

May this be possible? may this be true?

MELUN.

Have I not hideous death within my view,

Retaining but a quantity of life,

Which bleeds away even as a form of wax

Resolveth from his figure 'gainst the fire?

What in the world should make me now deceive,

Since I must lose the use of all deceit?

Why should I then be false, since it is true

That I must die here, and live hence by truth?

I say again, if Louis do will the day,

145

He is forsworn if e'er those eyes of yours

Behold another day break in the east:

But even this night,—whose black contagious breath

Already smokes about the burning crest

Of the old, feeble, and day-wearied sun,—

Even this ill night, your breathing shall expire;

Paying the fine of rated treachery

Even with a treacherous fine of all your lives,

If Louis by your assistance win the day.

Commend me to one Hubert, with your king;

The love of him,—and this respect besides,

For that my grandsire was an Englishman,—

Awakes my conscience to confess all this.

In lieu whereof, I pray you, bear me hence

From forth the noise and rumour of the field,

Where I may think the remnant of my thoughts

In peace, and part this body and my soul

With contemplation and devout desires.

SALISBURY.

We do believe thee:—and beshrew my soul

But I do love the favour and the form

Of this most fair occasion, by the which

We will untread the steps of damned flight;

And like a bated and retired flood,

Leaving our rankness and irregular course,

Stoop low within those bounds we have o'erlook'd,

And calmly run on in obedience

Even to our ocean, to our great King John.—

My arm shall give thee help to bear thee hence;

For I do see the cruel pangs of death

Right in thine eye.—Away, my friends! New flight,

And happy newness, that intends old right.

[Exeunt, leading off MELUN.]

SCENE 5. The same. The French camp.

[Enter LEWIS and his train.]

LOUIS.

The sun of heaven, methought, was loath to set,

But stay'd, and made the western welkin blush,

When the English measur'd backward their own ground

In faint retire. O, bravely came we off,

When with a volley of our needless shot,

After such bloody toil, we bid good night;

And wound our tattrring colours clearly up,

Last in the field, and almost lords of it!

[Enter a MESSENGER.]

MESSENGER.

Where is my prince, the Dauphin?

LOUIS.

Here:—what news?

MESSENGER.

The Count Melun is slain; the English lords

By his persuasion are again falln off:

And your supply, which you have wish'd so long,

Are cast away and sunk on Goodwin Sands.

LOUIS.

Ah, foul shrewd news!—beshrew thy very heart!—

I did not think to be so sad to-night

As this hath made me.—Who was he that said

King John did fly an hour or two before

The stumbling night did part our weary powers?

MESSENGER.

Whoever spoke it, it is true, my lord.

LOUIS.

Keep good quarter and good care to-night;

The day shall not be up so soon as I,

To try the fair adventure of to-morrow.

[Exeunt.]

SCENE 6. An open place in the neighborhood of Swinstead Abbey.

[Enter the BASTARD and HUBERT, meeting.]

HUBERT.

Who's there? speak, ho! speak quickly, or I shoot.

BASTARD.

A friend.—What art thou?

HUBERT.

Of the part of England.

BASTARD.

Whither dost thou go?

HUBERT.

What's that to thee? Why may I not demand

Of thine affairs, as well as thou of mine?

BASTARD.

Hubert, I think.

HUBERT.

Thou hast a perfect thought:

I will, upon all hazards, well believe

Thou art my friend that know'st my tongue so well.

Who art thou?

BASTARD.

Who thou wilt: and if thou please,

Thou mayst befriend me so much as to think

I come one way of the Plantagenets.

HUBERT.

Unkind remembrance! thou and eyeless night

Have done me shame:—brave soldier, pardon me,

That any accent breaking from thy tongue

Should scape the true acquaintance of mine ear.

BASTARD.

Come, come; sans compliment, what news abroad?

HUBERT.

Why, here walk I, in the black brow of night,

To find you out.

BASTARD.

Brief, then; and what's the news?

HUBERT.

O, my sweet sir, news fitting to the night,

Black, fearful, comfortless, and horrible.

BASTARD.

Show me the very wound of this ill news;

I am no woman, I'll not swoon at it.

HUBERT.

The king, I fear, is poison'd by a monk:

I left him almost speechless and broke out

To acquaint you with this evil, that you might

The better arm you to the sudden time,

Than if you had at leisure known of this.

BASTARD.

How did he take it; who did taste to him?

HUBERT.

A monk, I tell you; a resolved villain,

Whose bowels suddenly burst out: the king

Yet speaks, and peradventure may recover.

BASTARD.

Who didst thou leave to tend his majesty?

HUBERT.

Why, know you not? The lords are all come back,

And brought Prince Henry in their company;

At whose request the king hath pardon'd them,

And they are all about his majesty.

BASTARD.

Withhold thine indignation, mighty heaven,

And tempt us not to bear above our power!—

I'll tell thee, Hubert, half my power this night,

Passing these flats, are taken by the tide,—

These Lincoln washes have devoured them;

Myself, well-mounted, hardly have escap'd.

Away, before! conduct me to the king;

I doubt he will be dead or ere I come.

[Exeunt.]

SCENE 7. The orchard of Swinstead Abbey.

[Enter PRINCE HENRY, SALISBURY, and BIGOT.]

PRINCE HENRY.

It is too late: the life of all his blood

Is touch'd corruptibly, and his pure brain,—

Which some suppose the soul's frail dwelling-house,—

Doth, by the idle comments that it makes,

Foretell the ending of mortality.

[Enter PEMBROKE.]

PEMBROKE.

His Highness yet doth speak; and holds belief

That, being brought into the open air,

It would allay the burning quality

Of that fell poison which assaileth him.

PRINCE HENRY.

Let him be brought into the orchard here.—

Doth he still rage?

[Exit BIGOT.]

PEMBROKE.

He is more patient

Than when you left him; even now he sung.

PRINCE HENRY.

O vanity of sickness! fierce extremes

In their continuance will not feel themselves.

Death, having prey'd upon the outward parts,

Leaves them invisible; and his siege is now

Against the mind, the which he pricks and wounds

With many legions of strange fantasies,

Which, in their throng and press to that last hold,

Confound themselves. 'Tis strange that death should sing.—

I am the cygnet to this pale faint swan,

Who chants a doleful hymn to his own death;

And from the organ-pipe of frailty sings

His soul and body to their lasting rest.

SALISBURY.

Be of good comfort, prince; for you are born

To set a form upon that indigest

Which he hath left so shapeless and so rude.

[Re-enter BIGOT and Attendants, who bring in KING JOHN in a chair.]

KING JOHN.

Ay, marry, now my soul hath elbow-room;

It would not out at windows nor at doors.

There is so hot a summer in my bosom

That all my bowels crumble up to dust;

I am a scribbled form, drawn with a pen,

Upon a parchment; and against this fire

Do I shrink up.

PRINCE HENRY.

How fares your majesty?

KING JOHN.

Poison'd,—ill-fare;—dead, forsook, cast off;

And none of you will bid the winter come,

To thrust his icy fingers in my maw;

Nor let my kingdom's rivers take their course

Through my burn'd bosom; nor entreat the north

To make his bleak winds kiss my parched lips,

And comfort me with cold:—I do not ask you much;

I beg cold comfort; and you are so strait,

And so ingrateful, you deny me that.

PRINCE HENRY.

O, that there were some virtue in my tears,

That might relieve you!

KING JOHN.

The salt in them is hot.—

Within me is a hell; and there the poison

Is, as a fiend, confin'd to tyrannize

On unreprievable condemned blood.

[Enter the BASTARD.]

BASTARD.

O, I am scalded with my violent motion

And spleen of speed to see your majesty!

KING JOHN.

O cousin, thou art come to set mine eye:

The tackle of my heart is crack'd and burn'd;

And all the shrouds, wherewith my life should sail,

Are turned to one thread, one little hair:

My heart hath one poor string to stay it by,

Which holds but till thy news be uttered;

And then all this thou seest is but a clod,

And module of confounded royalty.

BASTARD.

The Dauphin is preparing hitherward,

Where heaven he knows how we shall answer him;

For in a night the best part of my power,

As I upon advantage did remove,

Were in the washes all unwarily

Devoured by the unexpected flood.

[The KING dies.]

SALISBURY.

You breathe these dead news in as dead an ear.

My liege! my lord!—But now a king,—now thus.

PRINCE HENRY.

Even so must I run on, and even so stop.

What surety of the world, what hope, what stay,

When this was now a king, and now is clay?

BASTARD.

Art thou gone so? I do but stay behind

To do the office for thee of revenge,

And then my soul shall wait on thee to heaven,

As it on earth hath been thy servant still.—

Now, now, you stars that move in your right spheres,

Where be your powers? Show now your mended faiths;

And instantly return with me again,

To push destruction and perpetual shame

Out of the weak door of our fainting land.

Straight let us seek, or straight we shall be sought;

The Dauphin rages at our very heels.

SALISBURY.

It seems you know not, then, so much as we:

The Cardinal Pandulph is within at rest,

Who half an hour since came from the Dauphin,

And brings from him such offers of our peace

As we with honour and respect may take,

With purpose presently to leave this war.

BASTARD.

He will the rather do it when he sees

Ourselves well sinewed to our defence.

SALISBURY.

Nay, 'tis in a manner done already;

For many carriages he hath despatch'd

To the sea-side, and put his cause and quarrel

To the disposing of the cardinal:

With whom yourself, myself, and other lords,

If you think meet, this afternoon will post

To consummate this business happily.

BASTARD.

Let it be so:—And you, my noble prince,

With other princes that may best be spar'd,

Shall wait upon your father's funeral.

PRINCE HENRY.

At Worcester must his body be interr'd;

For so he will'd it.

BASTARD.

Thither shall it, then:

And happily may your sweet self put on

The lineal state and glory of the land!

To whom, with all submission, on my knee,

I do bequeath my faithful services

And true subjection everlastingly.

SALISBURY.

And the like tender of our love we make,

To rest without a spot for evermore.

PRINCE HENRY.

I have a kind soul that would give you thanks,

And knows not how to do it but with tears.

BASTARD.

O, let us pay the time but needful woe,

Since it hath been beforehand with our griefs.—

This England never did, nor never shall,

Lie at the proud foot of a conqueror,

But when it first did help to wound itself.

Now these her princes are come home again,

Come the three corners of the world in arms,

And we shall shock them: nought shall make us rue,

If England to itself do rest but true.

[Exeunt.]

About Author

Shakespeare produced most of his known works between 1589 and 1613. His early plays were primarily comedies and histories and are regarded as some of the best work produced in these genres. Until about 1608, he wrote mainly tragedies, among them Hamlet, Othello, King Lear, and Macbeth, all considered to be among the finest works in the English language. In the last phase of his life, he wrote tragicomedies (also known as romances) and collaborated with other playwrights.

Many of Shakespeare's plays were published in editions of varying quality and accuracy in his lifetime. However, in 1623, two fellow actors and friends of Shakespeare's, John Heminges and Henry Condell, published a more definitive text known as the First Folio, a posthumous collected edition of Shakespeare's dramatic works that included all but two of his plays. The volume was prefaced with a poem by Ben Jonson, in which Jonson presciently hails Shakespeare in a now-famous quote as "not of an age, but for all time".

Throughout the 20th and 21st centuries, Shakespeare's works have been continually adapted and rediscovered by new movements in scholarship and performance. His plays remain popular and are studied, performed, and reinterpreted through various cultural and political contexts around the world.

Early life

William Shakespeare was the son of John Shakespeare, an alderman and a successful glover (glove-maker) originally from Snitterfield, and Mary Arden, the daughter of an affluent landowning farmer. He was born in Stratford-upon-Avon and baptised there on 26 April 1564. His actual date of birth remains unknown, but is traditionally observed on 23 April, Saint George's Day. This date, which can be traced to a mistake made by an 18th-century scholar, has proved appealing to biographers because Shakespeare died on the same date in 1616. He was the third of eight children, and the eldest surviving son.

Although no attendance records for the period survive, most biographers agree that Shakespeare was probably educated at the King's New School in Stratford, a free school chartered in 1553, about a quarter-mile (400 m) from his home. Grammar schools varied in quality during the Elizabethan era, but grammar school curricula were largely similar: the basic Latin text was standardised by royal decree, and the school would have provided an intensive education in grammar based upon Latin classical authors.

At the age of 18, Shakespeare married 26-year-old Anne Hathaway. The consistory court of the Diocese of Worcester issued a marriage licence on 27 November 1582. The next day, two of Hathaway's neighbours posted bonds guaranteeing that no lawful claims impeded the marriage. The ceremony may have been arranged in some haste since the Worcester chancellor allowed the marriage banns to be read once instead of the usual three times, and six months after the marriage Anne gave birth to a daughter, Susanna, baptised 26 May 1583. Twins, son Hamnet and daughter Judith, followed almost two years later and were baptised 2 February 1585. Hamnet died of unknown causes at the age of 11 and was buried 11 August 1596.

After the birth of the twins, Shakespeare left few historical traces until he is mentioned as part of the London theatre scene in 1592. The exception is the appearance of his name in the "complaints bill" of a law case before the Queen's Bench court at Westminster dated Michaelmas Term 1588 and 9 October 1589. Scholars refer to the years between 1585 and 1592 as Shakespeare's "lost years". Biographers attempting to account for this period have reported many apocryphal stories. Nicholas Rowe, Shakespeare's first biographer, recounted a Stratford legend that Shakespeare fled the town for London to escape prosecution for deer poaching in the estate of local squire Thomas Lucy. Shakespeare is also supposed to have taken his revenge on Lucy by writing a scurrilous ballad about him. Another 18th-century story has Shakespeare starting his theatrical career minding the horses of theatre patrons in London. John Aubrey reported that Shakespeare had been a country schoolmaster. Some 20th-century scholars have suggested that Shakespeare may have been employed as a schoolmaster by Alexander

Hoghton of Lancashire, a Catholic landowner who named a certain "William Shakeshafte" in his will. Little evidence substantiates such stories other than hearsay collected after his death, and Shakeshafte was a common name in the Lancashire area.

London and theatrical career

It is not known definitively when Shakespeare began writing, but contemporary allusions and records of performances show that several of his plays were on the London stage by 1592. By then, he was sufficiently known in London to be attacked in print by the playwright Robert Greene in his Groats-Worth of Wit:

... there is an upstart Crow, beautified with our feathers, that with his Tiger's heart wrapped in a Player's hide, supposes he is as well able to bombast out a blank verse as the best of you: and being an absolute Johannes factotum, is in his own conceit the only Shake-scene in a country.

Scholars differ on the exact meaning of Greene's words, but most agree that Greene was accusing Shakespeare of reaching above his rank in trying to match such university-educated writers as Christopher Marlowe, Thomas Nashe, and Greene himself (the so-called "University Wits"). The italicised phrase parodying the line "Oh, tiger's heart wrapped in a woman's hide" from Shakespeare's Henry VI, Part 3, along with the pun "Shake-scene", clearly identify Shakespeare as Greene's target. As used here, Johannes Factotum ("Jack of all trades") refers to a second-rate tinkerer with the work of others, rather than the more common "universal genius".

Greene's attack is the earliest surviving mention of Shakespeare's work in the theatre. Biographers suggest that his career may have begun any time from the mid-1580s to just before Greene's remarks. After 1594, Shakespeare's plays were performed only by the Lord Chamberlain's Men, a company owned by a group of players, including Shakespeare, that soon became the leading playing company in London. After the death of Queen Elizabeth in 1603, the company was awarded a royal patent by the new King James I, and changed its name to the King's Men.

"All the world's a stage,

and all the men and women merely players:

they have their exits and their entrances;

and one man in his time plays many parts ..."

—As You Like It, Act II, Scene 7, 139–142

In 1599, a partnership of members of the company built their own theatre on the south bank of the River Thames, which they named the Globe. In 1608, the partnership also took over the Blackfriars indoor theatre. Extant records of Shakespeare's property purchases and investments indicate that his association with the company made him a wealthy man, and in 1597, he bought the second-largest house in Stratford, New Place, and in 1605, invested in a share of the parish tithes in Stratford.

Some of Shakespeare's plays were published in quarto editions, beginning in 1594, and by 1598, his name had become a selling point and began to appear on the title pages. Shakespeare continued to act in his own and other plays after his success as a playwright. The 1616 edition of Ben Jonson's Works names him on the cast lists for Every Man in His Humour (1598) and Sejanus His Fall (1603). The absence of his name from the 1605 cast list for Jonson's Volpone is taken by some scholars as a sign that his acting career was nearing its end. The First Folio of 1623, however, lists Shakespeare as one of "the Principal Actors in all these Plays", some of which were first staged after Volpone, although we cannot know for certain which roles he played. In 1610, John Davies of Hereford wrote that "good Will" played "kingly" roles. In 1709, Rowe passed down a tradition that Shakespeare played the ghost of Hamlet's father. Later traditions maintain that he also played Adam in As You Like It, and the Chorus in Henry V, though scholars doubt the sources of that information.

Throughout his career, Shakespeare divided his time between London and Stratford. In 1596, the year before he bought New Place as his family home in Stratford, Shakespeare was living in the parish of St. Helen's, Bishopsgate, north of the River Thames. He moved across the river to Southwark by 1599, the same year his company constructed the Globe Theatre there. By 1604, he had moved north of the river again, to an area north of St Paul's Cathedral with many fine houses. There, he rented rooms from a French Huguenot named Christopher Mountjoy, a maker of ladies' wigs and other headgear.

Later years and death

Rowe was the first biographer to record the tradition, repeated by Johnson, that Shakespeare retired to Stratford "some years before his death". He was still working as an actor in London in 1608; in an answer to the sharers' petition in 1635, Cuthbert Burbage stated that after purchasing the lease of the Blackfriars Theatre in 1608 from Henry Evans, the King's Men "placed men players" there, "which were Heminges, Condell, Shakespeare, etc.". However, it is perhaps relevant that the bubonic plague raged in London throughout 1609. The London public playhouses were repeatedly closed during extended outbreaks of the plague (a total of over 60 months closure between May 1603 and February 1610), which meant there was often no acting work. Retirement from all work was uncommon at that time. Shakespeare continued to visit London during the years 1611–1614. In 1612, he was called as a witness in Bellott v. Mountjoy, a court case concerning the marriage settlement of Mountjoy's daughter, Mary. In March 1613, he bought a gatehouse in the former Blackfriars priory; and from November 1614, he was in London for several weeks with his son-in-law, John Hall. After 1610, Shakespeare wrote fewer plays, and none are attributed to him after 1613. His last three plays were collaborations, probably with John Fletcher, who succeeded him as the house playwright of the King's Men.

Shakespeare died on 23 April 1616, at the age of 52. He died within a month of signing his will, a document which he begins by describing himself as being in "perfect health". No extant contemporary source explains how or why he died. Half a century later, John Ward, the vicar of Stratford, wrote in his notebook: "Shakespeare, Drayton, and Ben Jonson had a merry meeting and, it seems, drank too hard, for Shakespeare died of a fever there contracted", not an impossible scenario since Shakespeare knew Jonson and Drayton. Of the tributes from fellow authors, one refers to his relatively sudden death: "We wondered, Shakespeare, that thou went'st so soon / From

167

the world's stage to the grave's tiring room."

He was survived by his wife and two daughters. Susanna had married a physician, John Hall, in 1607, and Judith had married Thomas Quiney, a vintner, two months before Shakespeare's death. Shakespeare signed his last will and testament on 25 March 1616; the following day, his new son-in-law, Thomas Quiney was found guilty of fathering an illegitimate son by Margaret Wheeler, who had died during childbirth. Thomas was ordered by the church court to do public penance, which would have caused much shame and embarrassment for the Shakespeare family.

Shakespeare bequeathed the bulk of his large estate to his elder daughter Susanna under stipulations that she pass it down intact to "the first son of her body". The Quineys had three children, all of whom died without marrying. The Halls had one child, Elizabeth, who married twice but died without children in 1670, ending Shakespeare's direct line. Shakespeare's will scarcely mentions his wife, Anne, who was probably entitled to one-third of his estate automatically. He did make a point, however, of leaving her "my second best bed", a bequest that has led to much speculation. Some scholars see the bequest as an insult to Anne, whereas others believe that the second-best bed would have been the matrimonial bed and therefore rich in significance.

Shakespeare was buried in the chancel of the Holy Trinity Church two days after his death. The epitaph carved into the stone slab covering his grave includes a curse against moving his bones, which was carefully avoided during restoration of the church in 2008:

Good frend for Iesvs sake forbeare,

To digg the dvst encloased heare.

Bleste be Middle English the.svg man Middle English that.svg spares thes stones,

And cvrst be he Middle English that.svg moves my bones.

(Modern spelling: Good friend, for Jesus' sake forbear, / To dig the dust enclosed here. / Blessed be the man that spares these stones, / And cursed be he that moves my bones.)

Some time before 1623, a funerary monument was erected in his memory on the north wall, with a half-effigy of him in the act of writing. Its plaque compares him to Nestor, Socrates, and Virgil. In 1623, in conjunction with the publication of the First Folio, the Droeshout engraving was published.

Shakespeare has been commemorated in many statues and memorials around the world, including funeral monuments in Southwark Cathedral and Poets' Corner in Westminster Abbey.

Plays

Most playwrights of the period typically collaborated with others at some point, and critics agree that Shakespeare did the same, mostly early and late in his career. Some attributions, such as Titus Andronicus and the early history plays, remain controversial while The Two Noble Kinsmen and the lost Cardenio have well-attested contemporary documentation. Textual evidence also supports the view that several of the plays were revised by other writers after their original composition.

The first recorded works of Shakespeare are Richard III and the three parts of Henry VI, written in the early 1590s during a vogue for historical drama. Shakespeare's plays are difficult to date precisely, however, and studies of the texts suggest that Titus Andronicus, The Comedy of Errors, The Taming of the Shrew, and The Two Gentlemen of Verona may also belong to Shakespeare's earliest period. His first histories, which draw heavily on the 1587 edition of Raphael Holinshed's Chronicles of England, Scotland, and Ireland, dramatise the destructive results of weak or corrupt rule and have been interpreted as a justification for the origins of the Tudor dynasty. The early plays were influenced by the works of other Elizabethan dramatists, especially Thomas Kyd and Christopher Marlowe, by the traditions of medieval drama, and by the plays of Seneca. The Comedy of Errors was also based on classical models, but no source for The Taming of the Shrew has been found, though it is related to a separate play of the same name and may have derived from a folk story. Like The Two Gentlemen of Verona, in which two friends appear to approve of rape, the Shrew's story of the taming of a woman's independent spirit by a man sometimes troubles modern critics, directors, and audiences.

Shakespeare's early classical and Italianate comedies, containing tight double plots and precise comic sequences, give way in the mid-1590s to the romantic atmosphere of his most acclaimed comedies. A Midsummer Night's Dream is a witty mixture of romance, fairy magic, and comic lowlife scenes. Shakespeare's next comedy, the equally romantic Merchant of Venice, contains a portrayal of the vengeful Jewish moneylender Shylock, which reflects Elizabethan views but may appear derogatory to modern audiences. The wit and wordplay of Much Ado About Nothing, the charming rural setting of As You Like It, and the lively merrymaking of Twelfth Night complete Shakespeare's sequence of great comedies. After the lyrical Richard II, written almost entirely in verse, Shakespeare introduced prose comedy into the histories of the late 1590s, Henry IV, parts 1 and 2, and Henry V. His characters become more complex and tender as he switches deftly between comic and serious scenes, prose and poetry, and achieves the narrative variety of his mature work. This period begins and ends with two tragedies: Romeo and Juliet, the famous romantic tragedy of sexually charged adolescence, love, and death; and Julius Caesar—based on Sir Thomas North's 1579 translation of Plutarch's Parallel Lives—which introduced a new kind of drama. According to Shakespearean scholar James Shapiro, in Julius Caesar, "the various strands of politics, character, inwardness, contemporary events, even Shakespeare's own reflections on the act of writing, began to infuse each other".

In the early 17th century, Shakespeare wrote the so-called "problem plays" Measure for Measure, Troilus and Cressida, and All's Well That Ends Well and a number of his best known tragedies. Many critics believe that Shakespeare's greatest tragedies represent the peak of his art. The titular hero of one of Shakespeare's greatest tragedies, Hamlet, has probably been discussed more than any other Shakespearean character, especially for his famous soliloquy which begins "To be or not to be; that is the question". Unlike the introverted Hamlet, whose fatal flaw is hesitation, the heroes of the tragedies that followed, Othello and King Lear, are undone by hasty errors of judgement. The plots of Shakespeare's tragedies often hinge on such fatal errors or flaws, which overturn order and destroy the hero and those he loves. In Othello, the villain Iago stokes Othello's sexual jealousy to the point where he murders the innocent wife who loves him. In King Lear, the old king commits the tragic error of giving up his powers, initiating the events which lead to the torture and blinding of the Earl of Gloucester and the murder of Lear's youngest daughter Cordelia. According to the critic Frank Kermode, "the play-offers neither its good characters nor its audience any relief from its cruelty". In Macbeth, the shortest and most compressed of Shakespeare's tragedies, uncontrollable ambition incites Macbeth and his wife, Lady Macbeth, to murder the rightful king and usurp the throne until their own guilt destroys them in turn. In this play, Shakespeare adds a supernatural element to the tragic structure. His last major tragedies, Antony and Cleopatra and Coriolanus, contain some of Shakespeare's finest poetry and were considered his most successful tragedies by the poet and critic T.S. Eliot.

In his final period, Shakespeare turned to romance or tragicomedy and completed three more major plays: Cymbeline, The Winter's Tale, and The Tempest, as well as the collaboration, Pericles, Prince of Tyre. Less bleak than the tragedies, these four plays are graver in tone than the comedies of the 1590s, but they end with reconciliation and the forgiveness of potentially tragic errors. Some commentators have seen this change in mood as evidence of a more serene view of life on Shakespeare's part, but it may merely reflect the theatrical fashion of the day. Shakespeare collaborated on two further surviving plays, Henry VIII and The Two Noble Kinsmen, probably with John Fletcher.

Performances

It is not clear for which companies Shakespeare wrote his early plays. The title page of the 1594 edition of Titus Andronicus reveals that the play had been acted by three different troupes. After the plagues of 1592–3, Shakespeare's plays were performed by his own company at The Theatre and the Curtain in Shoreditch, north of the Thames. Londoners flocked there to see the first part of Henry IV, Leonard Digges recording, "Let but Falstaff come, Hal, Poins, the rest ... and you scarce shall have a room". When the company found themselves in dispute with their landlord, they pulled The

Theatre down and used the timbers to construct the Globe Theatre, the first playhouse built by actors for actors, on the south bank of the Thames at Southwark. The Globe opened in autumn 1599, with Julius Caesar one of the first plays staged. Most of Shakespeare's greatest post-1599 plays were written for the Globe, including Hamlet, Othello, and King Lear.

After the Lord Chamberlain's Men were renamed the King's Men in 1603, they entered a special relationship with the new King James. Although the performance records are patchy, the King's Men performed seven of Shakespeare's plays at court between 1 November 1604, and 31 October 1605, including two performances of The Merchant of Venice. After 1608, they performed at the indoor Blackfriars Theatre during the winter and the Globe during the summer. The indoor setting, combined with the Jacobean fashion for lavishly staged masques, allowed Shakespeare to introduce more elaborate stage devices. In Cymbeline, for example, Jupiter descends "in thunder and lightning, sitting upon an eagle: he throws a thunderbolt. The ghosts fall on their knees."

The actors in Shakespeare's company included the famous Richard Burbage, William Kempe, Henry Condell and John Heminges. Burbage played the leading role in the first performances of many of Shakespeare's plays, including Richard III, Hamlet, Othello, and King Lear. The popular comic actor Will Kempe played the servant Peter in Romeo and Juliet and Dogberry in Much Ado About Nothing, among other characters. He was replaced around 1600 by Robert Armin, who played roles such as Touchstone in As You Like It and the fool in King Lear. In 1613, Sir Henry Wotton recorded that Henry VIII "was set forth with many extraordinary circumstances of pomp and ceremony". On 29 June, however, a cannon set fire to the thatch of the Globe and burned the theatre to the ground, an event which pinpoints the date of a Shakespeare play with rare precision.

Textual sources

In 1623, John Heminges and Henry Condell, two of Shakespeare's friends from the King's Men, published the First Folio, a collected edition of Shakespeare's plays. It contained 36 texts, including 18 printed for the

172

first time. Many of the plays had already appeared in quarto versions—flimsy books made from sheets of paper folded twice to make four leaves. No evidence suggests that Shakespeare approved these editions, which the First Folio describes as "stol'n and surreptitious copies". Nor did Shakespeare plan or expect his works to survive in any form at all; those works likely would have faded into oblivion but for his friends' spontaneous idea, after his death, to create and publish the First Folio.

Alfred Pollard termed some of the pre-1623 versions as "bad quartos" because of their adapted, paraphrased or garbled texts, which may in places have been reconstructed from memory. Where several versions of a play survive, each differs from the other. The differences may stem from copying or printing errors, from notes by actors or audience members, or from Shakespeare's own papers. In some cases, for example, Hamlet, Troilus and Cressida, and Othello, Shakespeare could have revised the texts between the quarto and folio editions. In the case of King Lear, however, while most modern editions do conflate them, the 1623 folio version is so different from the 1608 quarto that the Oxford Shakespeare prints them both, arguing that they cannot be conflated without confusion.

Influence from neighbours in London

Ten years of research by Geoffrey Marsh (museum director) of the Victoria and Albert Museum in London may have shown that Shakespeare got many of the ideas and information for his plays, from his neighbours that he lived near in London in the late 1590s.

Geoffrey Marsh found the site of Shakespeare's house in St Helen's Church, Bishopsgate parish, at the corner of St.Helen's churchyard and Bishopsgate Street, north of the churchyard, from the records of the Leathersellers Company. Many wealthy and notable people (including Sir John Spencer and Dr. Edward Jorden and Dr. Peter Turner), with connections across Europe, lived near Shakespeare.

Poems

In 1593 and 1594, when the theatres were closed because of plague,

Shakespeare published two narrative poems on sexual themes, Venus and Adonis and The Rape of Lucrece. He dedicated them to Henry Wriothesley, Earl of Southampton. In Venus and Adonis, an innocent Adonis rejects the sexual advances of Venus; while in The Rape of Lucrece, the virtuous wife Lucrece is raped by the lustful Tarquin. Influenced by Ovid's Metamorphoses, the poems show the guilt and moral confusion that result from uncontrolled lust. Both proved popular and were often reprinted during Shakespeare's lifetime. A third narrative poem, A Lover's Complaint, in which a young woman laments her seduction by a persuasive suitor, was printed in the first edition of the Sonnets in 1609. Most scholars now accept that Shakespeare wrote A Lover's Complaint. Critics consider that its fine qualities are marred by leaden effects. The Phoenix and the Turtle, printed in Robert Chester's 1601 Love's Martyr, mourns the deaths of the legendary phoenix and his lover, the faithful turtle dove. In 1599, two early drafts of sonnets 138 and 144 appeared in The Passionate Pilgrim, published under Shakespeare's name but without his permission.

Sonnets

Published in 1609, the Sonnets were the last of Shakespeare's non-dramatic works to be printed. Scholars are not certain when each of the 154 sonnets was composed, but evidence suggests that Shakespeare wrote sonnets throughout his career for a private readership. Even before the two unauthorised sonnets appeared in The Passionate Pilgrim in 1599, Francis Meres had referred in 1598 to Shakespeare's "sugred Sonnets among his private friends". Few analysts believe that the published collection follows Shakespeare's intended sequence. He seems to have planned two contrasting series: one about uncontrollable lust for a married woman of dark complexion (the "dark lady"), and one about conflicted love for a fair young man (the "fair youth"). It remains unclear if these figures represent real individuals, or if the authorial "I" who addresses them represents Shakespeare himself, though Wordsworth believed that with the sonnets "Shakespeare unlocked his heart".

"Shall I compare thee to a summer's day?

Thou art more lovely and more temperate ..."

—Lines from Shakespeare's Sonnet 18.

The 1609 edition was dedicated to a "Mr. W.H.", credited as "the only begetter" of the poems. It is not known whether this was written by Shakespeare himself or by the publisher, Thomas Thorpe, whose initials appear at the foot of the dedication page; nor is it known who Mr. W.H. was, despite numerous theories, or whether Shakespeare even authorised the publication. Critics praise the Sonnets as a profound meditation on the nature of love, sexual passion, procreation, death, and time.

Style

Shakespeare's first plays were written in the conventional style of the day. He wrote them in a stylised language that does not always spring naturally from the needs of the characters or the drama. The poetry depends on extended, sometimes elaborate metaphors and conceits, and the language is often rhetorical—written for actors to declaim rather than speak. The grand speeches in Titus Andronicus, in the view of some critics, often hold up the action, for example; and the verse in The Two Gentlemen of Verona has been described as stilted.

However, Shakespeare soon began to adapt the traditional styles to his own purposes. The opening soliloquy of Richard III has its roots in the self-declaration of Vice in medieval drama. At the same time, Richard's vivid self-awareness looks forward to the soliloquies of Shakespeare's mature plays. No single play marks a change from the traditional to the freer style. Shakespeare combined the two throughout his career, with Romeo and Juliet perhaps the best example of the mixing of the styles. By the time of Romeo and Juliet, Richard II, and A Midsummer Night's Dream in the mid-1590s, Shakespeare had begun to write a more natural poetry. He increasingly tuned his metaphors and images to the needs of the drama itself.

Shakespeare's standard poetic form was blank verse, composed in iambic pentameter. In practice, this meant that his verse was usually unrhymed and consisted of ten syllables to a line, spoken with a stress on every second syllable. The blank verse of his early plays is quite different from that of his later ones. It is often beautiful, but its sentences tend to start, pause, and finish at the end of lines, with the risk of monotony. Once Shakespeare mastered traditional blank verse, he began to interrupt and vary its flow. This technique releases the new power and flexibility of the poetry in plays such as Julius Caesar and Hamlet. Shakespeare uses it, for example, to convey the turmoil in Hamlet's mind:

> Sir, in my heart there was a kind of fighting
>
> That would not let me sleep. Methought I lay
>
> Worse than the mutines in the bilboes. Rashly—
>
> And prais'd be rashness for it—let us know
>
> Our indiscretion sometimes serves us well ...
>
> —Hamlet, Act 5, Scene 2, 4–8

After Hamlet, Shakespeare varied his poetic style further, particularly in the more emotional passages of the late tragedies. The literary critic A. C. Bradley described this style as "more concentrated, rapid, varied, and, in construction, less regular, not seldom twisted or elliptical". In the last phase of his career, Shakespeare adopted many techniques to achieve these effects. These included run-on lines, irregular pauses and stops, and extreme variations in sentence structure and length. In Macbeth, for example, the language darts from one unrelated metaphor or simile to another: "was the hope drunk/ Wherein you dressed yourself?" (1.7.35–38); "... pity, like a naked new-born babe/ Striding the blast, or heaven's cherubim, hors'd/ Upon the sightless couriers of the air ..." (1.7.21–25). The listener is challenged to complete the sense. The late romances, with their shifts in time and surprising turns of plot, inspired a last poetic style in which long and short sentences are set against one another, clauses are piled up, subject and object are reversed, and words are omitted, creating an effect of spontaneity.

Shakespeare combined poetic genius with a practical sense of the theatre. Like all playwrights of the time, he dramatised stories from sources such as Plutarch and Holinshed. He reshaped each plot to create several centres of interest and to show as many sides of a narrative to the audience as

176

possible. This strength of design ensures that a Shakespeare play can survive translation, cutting and wide interpretation without loss to its core drama. As Shakespeare's mastery grew, he gave his characters clearer and more varied motivations and distinctive patterns of speech. He preserved aspects of his earlier style in the later plays, however. In Shakespeare's late romances, he deliberately returned to a more artificial style, which emphasised the illusion of theatre.

Influence

Shakespeare's work has made a lasting impression on later theatre and literature. In particular, he expanded the dramatic potential of characterisation, plot, language, and genre. Until Romeo and Juliet, for example, romance had not been viewed as a worthy topic for tragedy. Soliloquies had been used mainly to convey information about characters or events, but Shakespeare used them to explore characters' minds. His work heavily influenced later poetry. The Romantic poets attempted to revive Shakespearean verse drama, though with little success. Critic George Steiner described all English verse dramas from Coleridge to Tennyson as "feeble variations on Shakespearean themes."

Shakespeare influenced novelists such as Thomas Hardy, William Faulkner, and Charles Dickens. The American novelist Herman Melville's soliloquies owe much to Shakespeare; his Captain Ahab in Moby-Dick is a classic tragic hero, inspired by King Lear. Scholars have identified 20,000 pieces of music linked to Shakespeare's works. These include three operas by Giuseppe Verdi, Macbeth, Otello and Falstaff, whose critical standing compares with that of the source plays. Shakespeare has also inspired many painters, including the Romantics and the Pre-Raphaelites. The Swiss Romantic artist Henry Fuseli, a friend of William Blake, even translated Macbeth into German. The psychoanalyst Sigmund Freud drew on Shakespearean psychology, in particular, that of Hamlet, for his theories of human nature.

In Shakespeare's day, English grammar, spelling, and pronunciation were less standardised than they are now, and his use of language helped shape modern English. Samuel Johnson quoted him more often than any other author in his A Dictionary of the English Language, the first serious work of its type. Expressions such as "with bated breath" (Merchant of Venice) and "a foregone conclusion" (Othello) have found their way into everyday English speech.

Works

Classification of the plays

Shakespeare's works include the 36 plays printed in the First Folio of 1623, listed according to their folio classification as comedies, histories, and tragedies. Two plays not included in the First Folio, The Two Noble Kinsmen and Pericles, Prince of Tyre, are now accepted as part of the canon, with today's scholars agreeing that Shakespeare made major contributions to the writing of both. No Shakespearean poems were included in the First Folio.

In the late 19th century, Edward Dowden classified four of the late comedies as romances, and though many scholars prefer to call them tragicomedies, Dowden's term is often used. In 1896, Frederick S. Boas coined the term "problem plays" to describe four plays: All's Well That Ends Well, Measure for Measure, Troilus and Cressida, and Hamlet. "Dramas as singular in theme and temper cannot be strictly called comedies or tragedies", he wrote. "We may, therefore, borrow a convenient phrase from the theatre of today and class them together as Shakespeare's problem plays." The term, much debated and sometimes applied to other plays, remains in use, though Hamlet is definitively classed as a tragedy. (Source: Wikipedia)

CPSIA information can be obtained
at www.ICGtesting.com
Printed in the USA
BVHW030347170719
R10118200002B/R101182PG553580BVX3B/2